מעגל החיים

THE JEWISH LIFE CYCLE:
Rituals and Concepts

BASED ON A USY STUDY PROGRAM BY
RABBI SAM KIEFFER
Edited by Rabbi Stephen Garfinkel

UPDATED BY ARI YARES
EDITED BY KAREN L. STEIN

WITH CONTRIBUTIONS FROM EITAN GUTIN AND DAVID SREBNICK

UNITED SYNAGOGUE OF CONSERVATIVE JUDAISM
DEPARTMENT OF YOUTH ACTIVITIES

Jules A. Gutin, Director
Karen L. Stein, Education Director
Stephanie Goldsmith, Projects Coordinator
Ezra Androphy, Activities Coordinator
Hirsch Fishman, Publications Coordinator
Ilana Clay, Program Coordinator
Jeremy Luski, Manager of Meetings and Special Events
Yossi Garr, Central Shaliach
Sophie Fellman-Rafalovitz, West Coast Shlicha
Yitzchak Jacobsen, Director, Israel Office
David Keren, Director, Israel Programs

INTERNATIONAL YOUTH COMMISSION
Robert Sunshine, Co-Chair
Dr. Marilyn Lishnoff Wind, Co-Chair

UNITED SYNAGOGUE OF CONSERVATIVE JUDAISM
Judy Yudof, International President
Rabbi Jerome M. Epstein, Executive Vice President

A publication of the International Youth Commission
United Synagogue of Conservative Judaism
155 Fifth Avenue, New York, NY 10010
www.usy.org

Printed and bound in the United States of America by Phoenix Color Corp.

Cover design by Hirsch Fishman

Production, layout and design by Karen L. Stein, Project Editor

In memory

אליעזר יאיר בן הרב גרשון ושולמית ז"ל

Eliezer "Elie" Schwartz

International USY Religion/ Education Vice President 1999

With thanks to our readers

Rabbi Jerome M. Epstein
Jonathan Greenberg
Eitan Gutin
Jules Gutin
Rabbi Eliot Marrus
David Srebnick

For many contributions and assistance

This book contains sacred text and should be treated with appropriate respect.

TABLE OF CONTENTS

introduction

By Rabbi Sam Kieffer

We Jews are an optimistic people. We always assume that things are not as bad as they seem, and that tomorrow will always be better than today. This is one of the factors that led to the belief in the Messianic Age: our hope that there will be a time when the world is at peace and when love and harmony reign in the universe. This helps explain the importance we attach to the ceremonies and rituals of the life cycle of the Jew. By celebrating these events in the life of every Jew, we proclaim that no matter what the external conditions may be, we Jews can find something about which to celebrate and rejoice. It takes an optimistic people to perform a *brit milah* (circumcision) in a concentration camp; that act assumes that although life in the camp is temporary, living as a Jew is valued as something eternal, and that Jewish values will survive long after the camps are relegated to dust and ashes.

Secondly, Jews have a sense of history. While we look optimistically and hopefully to the future, our vision is framed and focused by the experiences of our collective past. Jewish ritual places the individual not only in the perspective of sociology—namely, where he belongs within his people—but also in the perspective of history. It is sobering to consider that no matter what the conditions were—from Jewish self-government, to inquisitions, to Nazi concentration camps—whenever possible, the Jewish male was circumcised, Jewish weddings took place, and Jewish burial procedures were strictly observed. There is a *midrash* that relates that during the revelation at Mount Sinai, the ears of every Jew who lived before and after that event were present. Through this *midrash*, the Rabbis were expressing the perception that the Jew identifies with each generation before and after him. By performing these rites of passage in a prescribed and uniform manner, we declare our devotion to tradition with the realization that the Jew has no future unless he knows and experiences his past.

Thirdly, Jews are tremendously concerned with the importance of each individual. Celebration of events throughout one's lifetime is our people's way of telling the individual, "You count for something. You are worthwhile. You are not just a face in the crowd." It is of tremendous psychological impact to dedicate an entire day to a thirteen-year-old boy or a twelve-year-old girl. At that age of adolescence, when a child is forming a self-image, an identity, just when the child is questioning, "Who am I?" the community gathers and tells him or her, "You are an important part of our people." In the case of death, we do not allow the individual to drown in an ocean of sorrow. We, the Jewish people, tell the mourner, "Go ahead and cry your heart out. Bewail the loss of your loved one. Afterwards, we will help you recover your sense of direction and purpose." The laws of mourning constitute a programmed plan for renormalization of the individual.

Fourthly, Jewish rituals concretize our sense of community. The uniformity with which these rituals are practiced instills within us a deep sense of unity and community with our fellow Jews, wherever they may be. In spite of the fact that a great deal of variation exists in the carrying out of so many of our practices, there are enough common strains to each of the life cycle ceremonies to view them as the common property of all Jews. Thus, whether one comes from Morocco, Israel, Poland, or North America, a Jew can automatically tell a Jewish wedding from a non-Jewish one, or identify a home as one in which a Jewish family is in mourning. It is inspiring to realize that a *brit milah* done in my home is essentially the same ceremony performed in a Jewish home across the globe.

The life cycle ceremonies thus fulfill at least four important tasks. They provide a cause for rejoicing, they provide a means for reinforcing our ties to tradition; they provide a means by which our society can emphasize the importance of each individual; and they concretize the unity of the Jewish people. Now that we know what ritual does, let us explore what ritual is.

Ritual involves action. The action must be done in essentially the same way every time it is done. It must be done either at a specified time, or as an automatic reaction to a preliminary set of circumstances. For example, one can light *Shabbat* candles on Thursday afternoon, but such an act would not be considered the ritual performance of lighting *Shabbat* candles. Or, one can tear one's clothes at any time, but the ritual of *keriah* (tearing) can only be considered as the religious ritual when done following the death of a family member. Finally, ritual has a symbolic meaning. There is some conceptual significance to an act that's has been labeled a ritual. During the course of a day, we perform many symbolic acts, usually without even realizing it. For instance, shaking hands upon greeting a person is something we do out of habit. However, this simple act does have significance. In ancient times, this act was an expression of peaceful intentions. A closed fist could conceal a weapon; an extended open hand revealed the absence of danger. Thus, when shaking hands, we may be saying, "It is a pleasure to meet you," but symbolically, we are also saying, "I come in peace; I do not intend to hurt you."

When a citizen salutes his nation's flag, he is not paying homage to the piece of cloth—that would be idolatry. (Some individuals do fall into that trap by taking loyalty to an extreme.) By saluting the flag, an individual is symbolically saluting the ideals of the nation represented by the flag.

In Judaism, we usually add one more ingredient to an action in order for it to be considered a ritual. We add a *bracha* or prayer of some sort—this serves to sanctify the act. Let us reflect upon the set of rituals that make up the *Shabbat*. The Kiddush expresses twin themes—*zaycher le'ma'asay braysheet* (remembering the creation of the world) and *zaycher le'yetziat Mitzrayim* (remembering the exodus from Egypt). When we consider that God used six days to create the contents of the universe, and a seventh day to "take stock," to evaluate it by letting it function on its own, we realize that this is our task too. At the same time, upon recalling our exodus from Egypt, we are reminded that the earth needs redemption also from the slavery of our technological oppression of its resources. By observing *Shabbat* as is prescribed by its rituals, we enter the rest of the week a little differently. We have a day to look forward to, a day to take account of our deeds and thoughts, and to replenish our energy supply in order to face our tasks anew. This is what the late Abraham Joshua Heschel meant when he said that on *Shabbat*, "we go from the world of creation to the creation of the world." By symbolically commemorating the *Ma'asay Beraysheet*, we are inspired to resolve to create new worlds each week—new ambitions, new plans, and new vigor with which to carry them out. When we use the term "rest" to describe what kind of day *Shabbat* is, we mean that we are putting to rest our inaction, our laziness, our rationalizations. We are exorcising the demons of complacency and indifference to the magnificence of this universe and all the promise it holds for the true and lasting exodus of a free mankind.

What *Shabbat* does for the week, the life cycle ceremonies do for the individual's lifetime. These rituals are our attempt to make meaning and significance out of existence. We can now turn to an analysis of the specific rituals involved in the life cycle of the Jew.

1) Explore the "problem" of traditions—the conclusion that our rituals have inherent value comes after study and interpretation to get to the root of the practice under discussion. What if after lengthy study, we conclude that there does not seem to be a valid reason or purpose to ritual anymore? A logical conclusion might be that the practice should be dropped. Or should we continue to observe it on the assumption that if it lasted so many years, perhaps it is <u>our</u> perception that is faulty, not the practice?

2) An area of concern for teenagers, in particular, is the fear of a "robot mentality," i.e., that ritual can become too mechanical by being done the same way each time. Is there room for variation within a ritual practice? Is there a value in doing something the same way each time? Is there room for variation with a prescribed ritual practice?

3) What are the major Jewish life cycle events? Do you see any similarities between these rituals and those of other cultures?

4) Why is it important to celebrate life cycle events?

5) Are there occasions in the life of a Jew that should be marked by life cycle rituals, other than the ones presently observed? Should we create new ones?

1. Where are you in life right now?

2. Where do you plan to go next?

3. How do you use your connection to Judaism in making these decisions?

4. My most meaningful Jewish experience to date has been…

Before completing the lifeline on the next page, please answer these questions:

LOOKING BACK

What have been the milestones in your life up until now?

Which are Jewishly related?

Which aren't?

Were there different celebrations depending on which were and were not Jewish milestones?

Now, complete the lifeline on the next page.

Questions for discussion, after filling in the Jewish lifelines:

Which milestones do you agree with on each timeline? Which do you disagree with?

Are you looking forward to anything on the North American timeline? What? Why?

Are you looking forward to anything on the Jewish timeline? What? Why?

Take a look at both timelines. Are there any milestones you would move to a different age? Are there any milestones that you would remove entirely? Why?

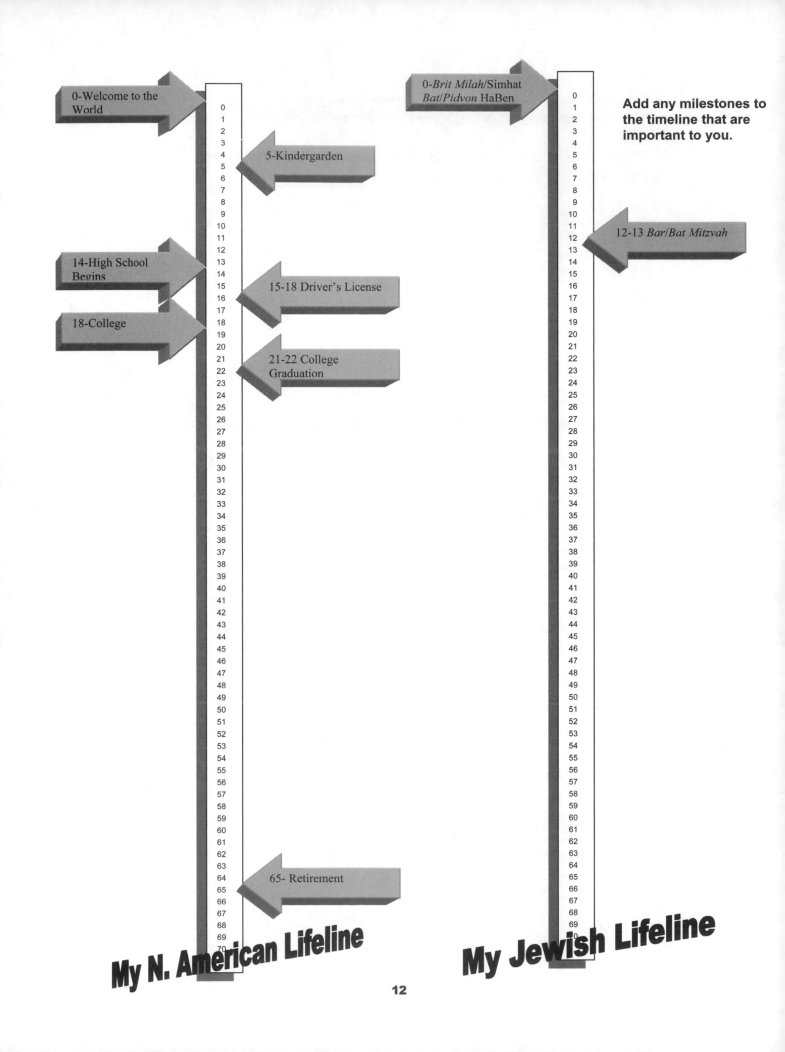

0-Welcome to the World

5-Kindergarden

14-High School Begins

15-18 Driver's License

18-College

21-22 College Graduation

65- Retirement

My N. American Lifeline

0-*Brit Milah*/Simhat *Bat*/*Pidvon* HaBen

Add any milestones to the timeline that are important to you.

12-13 *Bar/Bat Mitzvah*

My Jewish Lifeline

rituals of birth

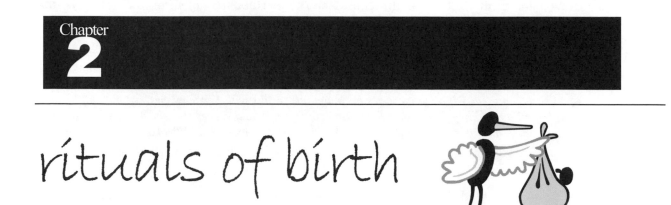

THE OBLIGATION TO HAVE CHILDREN[1]

Birth plays a central role in Judaism. The first words that God spoke to humanity include the instruction to have children.

וַיְבָרֶךְ אֹתָם אֱלֹהִים וַיֹּאמֶר לָהֶם אֱלֹהִים פְּרוּ וּרְבוּ וּמִלְאוּ אֶת־הָאָרֶץ
וְכִבְשֻׁהָ וּרְדוּ בִּדְגַת הַיָּם וּבְעוֹף הַשָּׁמַיִם וּבְכָל־חַיָּה הָרֹמֶשֶׂת עַל־הָאָרֶץ:

God blessed them and God said to them, "Be fertile and increase, fill the earth and master it; and rule the fish of the sea, the birds of the sky, and all the living things that creep on the earth." (Bereishit 1:28)

The fact that the first *mitzvah* mentioned in the Torah has to do with procreation is not to be taken lightly. It is a fundamental obligation for every Jew to try to have children. So central is this desire that the inability of a spouse to have children was considered grounds for divorce. While it is difficult to determine how frequently this scenario was played out, it still says something about Judaism's recognition of its minority status in the world and about its attitude towards the importance of procreation. The "complete" Jewish life is perceived as one which includes marriage and the fulfillment of the precept of "Be fruitful and multiply."

That is not to say that one cannot be a good Jew without being married, for whatever reason. Nor does it say that couples who are infertile are seen as a hindrance to our people. Our religion is neither insensitive to those who have not succeeded in finding a fitting partner nor cruel to those who have been dealt a trying hand. It does however illuminate an ideal which a Jew should strive to achieve.

Judaism's concern is not necessarily for personal fulfillment, although there may be no greater one than having a child, but rather upon the need for each and every Jew to concern him or herself with national fulfillment. The Jew should never view his or her existence in a vacuum. What one does as an individual has significant ramifications for all Jews. The nation moves forward only as a result of the efforts of individuals, of people being concerned for the greater Jewish community. This, perhaps more than anything, is the ethic which the commandment of procreation expresses.

---

[1] Excerpted from We Are Family, Rabbi Joel Wasser, United Synagogue of Conservative Judaism, Dept of Youth Activities, 1991

Having stated that, it is worth considering the Rabbinic interpretation of how the commandment of reproduction is fulfilled, as found in *Yevamot* 6:7:

> *One cannot desist from the mitzvah of procreation unless one already has children. The disciples of Shammai define this as having had two sons. The disciples of Hillel define this as having had a son and a daughter, as it is stated in Bereishit 5:2, "Male and female, God created them." If a man marries a woman and dwells with her ten years without children, he should not desist from trying to fulfill the mitzvah. If he divorces her, she may marry someone else. A man is commanded to procreate, but not a woman. Rabbi Broka states that both are obligated, as it is written, "And God blessed them and said to them... be fruitful and multiply."*

The passage quoted illustrates several ideas, one an important methodological point in Rabbinic Judaism. The rabbis often prove things are true by quoting the Bible. A fact is only as true as its textual basis. Once a verse is established, however, a point is irrefutable. In the rabbinic mind, what could be more convincing than a verse from Scripture? The Holy word is certainly proof. Nonetheless, as our dispute implies, even this methodology is not without conflict.

While the disciples of Hillel look to God's creation of mankind to support their position, the disciples of Shammai look to the ultimate teacher, Moses, to prove their point, for Moses had two sons. While one opinion looks to the conclusion of the Biblical verse, "Be fruitful and multiply, fill the land <u>and subdue it</u>," and suggestions that it is the man whose character it is to subdue and thus his *mitzvah* only, another looks to the beginning of the verse and its plural form to support that the *mitzvah* is equally incumbent upon both males and females. Suffice it to say, that no matter how it is precisely explained, the command for a husband and wife to create life represents a most fundamental and integral aspect of Judaism. Again, one cannot preserve an ideology should one not create beings to adhere to it.

This first *mitzvah* drives the life cycle events that will be discussed throughout this book.

1) **Why do you think God seems to be commanding Adam and Eve to "be fertile and increase?" Shouldn't this be the only obvious way to preserve humankind?**

2) **What are the reasons that parents choose to have children? What do you think the positive parts of being a parent are? What are the difficult parts?**

3) **Do you think your parents "owe" you anything beyond the fact that they gave you life? What minimum things do you expect from them? List the three most important.**

הוּא הָיָה אוֹמֵר, יָפָה שָׁעָה אַחַת בִּתְשׁוּבָה וּמַעֲשִׂים טוֹבִים בָּעוֹלָם הַזֶּה, מִכָּל חַיֵּי הָעוֹלָם הַבָּא. וְיָפָה שָׁעָה אַחַת שֶׁל קוֹרַת רוּחַ בָּעוֹלָם הַבָּא, מִכָּל חַיֵּי הָעוֹלָם הַזֶּה:

Rabbi Shimon taught: There are three crowns: the crown of Torah, the crown of Priesthood, the crown of Royalty. The crown of a good name is superior to them all. (Pirke Avot 4:7)

LOOKING BACK

1. **What is your name in Hebrew and English?**

2. **Do you know the meaning of your name?**

3. **What are the reasons you were given this name?**

4. **What are the other things you are called besides your given name?**

Who are you? Most of us probably answer that question by giving our name. Some people have more than one name. That second name may be a nickname given to them by friends or family or it may be a shortened form of their first or last name. Having a name gives you a sense of identity and gaining a name is one of the first ways that we, as individuals, make our presence known in the world (aside from all the crying after we are born). The second question asked when we hear that someone has had a baby (the first question is whether it is a boy or a girl) is often, "What is his or her name?" Names are so fundamentally important in our society that you cannot leave the hospital without one (although some children have gone home as "Baby Schwartz").

As Jews, we also have a Hebrew name by which we can identify ourselves. For some people, this name may be the same or similar to their English name. For others, it may be completely different. Depending upon your family's background, this name may be from a deceased relative whom your parents wished to memorialize if you are *Ashkenazi* (of Central and Eastern European descent), or if you are *Sephardi*, (of Spanish or Mediterranean descent) then your name may be from a living relative whom your parents wished to honor. Sometimes, the exact same name is used or a name that starts with the same letter (e.g. Michael for Morris).[2]

Unlike in a North American hospital where a nurse or clerk may ask your parent what your name is so that it may be written on your birth certificate, receiving a Jewish name involves much celebration and ritual. The ceremony or ceremonies that accompany your birth and naming differ depending upon gender and Jewish heritage. We'll begin with *brit milah*, the ritual for boys, and then continue with *Simchat Bat* and other ceremonies for girls.

1. **Why is your name important to you?**

2. **If you had a choice of a name for yourself what name would you come up with?**

---

[2] How does a Hebrew name work?
Last names are a relatively modern invention. In Judaism, your full name is composed of your first name and middle name (e.g. Ari Shlomo) followed by *ben* (son of) or *Bat* (daughter of) and then your parents' Hebrew names. If your father is a *Kohen* (priest) or a *Levite*, then you would add "ha-*Kohen*" or "ha-*Levi*" at the end of your name.

Hebrew names are used in the following religious occasions:

- When called to the Torah for an *aliyah*

- When one prays for someone who is ill

- *Bar* and *Bat Mitzvah* ceremony

- When signing the *Ketubah* (marriage contract as a witness)

- At a funeral, burial, and when saying *Yizkor*

- When the parents bless their children on *Shabbat*.

BRIT MILAH   סדר ברית מילה

According to our tradition, there are things that occur immediately after birth which a parent is obligated to provide for a child. The following passage from the Talmud, *Kiddushin* 29a, gives a list:

האב חייב בבנו למולו, ולפדותו, וללמדו תורה, ולהשיאו אשה, וללמדו
אומנות וי"א: אף להשיטו במים

A father is obligated to do the following for his son: to circumcise him, to redeem him if he is a first-born, to teach him Torah, to find him a wife, and to teach him a trade. There are those who say to teach him to swim.

Keeping in mind the ancient context of the Talmud, in contrast to today's reality of more equality between males and females, some might argue for a broader rephrasing of the text: A <u>parent</u> is obligated to do the following for one's <u>child</u>. Let's look together at the first two obligations in the list:

- To enter the child into the covenant (this might include a *Simchat HaBat* ceremony for girls as well as circumcision for the boys)

- To redeem him if he is a first-born (the *mitzvah* of *Pidyon HaBen* does not apply to females).

Entering the Covenant: Whether speaking of a baby boy or girl, perhaps no ceremony holds as much significance for a family as one which formalizes one's child entering into the covenant. From that point on, the baby is no longer just a baby, but rather a descendant of *Avraham Avinu*, Abraham our Father, and *Sarah Emanu*, Sarah our Mother. Through this ceremony shortly after birth, a significant statement is made about nationhood. Through the covenant ceremony, the family proclaims that both the joy of the infant's birth and indeed the infant him or herself, belong not only to the immediate family, but indeed to the entire people of Israel. Entering the covenant echoes many ideas, not the least of which is the fact that another Jew has entered the world and that our entire people should rejoice. By engaging in this act one concretizes the recognition that as a Jew, the individual is part of a greater whole and that one's destiny is measured not just in terms of personal fulfillment but in terms of national success as well.

Redeeming: the act of *Pidyon HaBen*, the redeeming of the mother's first-born child, is a precept which applies to male children only. It serves as a remembrance of the flight from Egypt and the fact that while God executed judgment upon all male first-borns in Egypt, from mankind to animal, the Israelite males were spared. From that point forward, all first-born males were consecrated to God. It was only through the redemption ceremony that a family actually acquired the first-born male from God. Fundamental to this ceremony is the concretization of a historical conscience. By remembering the events in Egypt and by performing a ritual commanded within that context, the Jew ties his or her personal past into that of the national past. One says: I am a continuation of that history which is a part of my people. I do not live in a temporal vacuum, rather, I am a link in the ever unfolding destiny of the greater Jewish people.

How is the brit milah...

A Cause For Rejoicing	Something that tied me to tradition	Something that made me feel important	Something that helps Jewish unity

Brit Milah (or *bris* if using an Ashkenazi pronunciation) literally translates as covenant of circumcision. *Brit Milah*, however, is more than just a ritual circumcision. The Bible, in the texts below, portrays the rite as having begun with Abraham.[3]

יא וּנְמַלְתֶּם אֵת בְּשַׂר עָרְלַתְכֶם וְהָיָה לְאוֹת בְּרִית בֵּינִי וּבֵינֵיכֶם:

You shall circumcise the flesh of your foreskin, and that shall be the sign of the covenant between Me and you. (*Bereishit 17:11*)

1. **What, according to the text, is the origin of the commandment for Jews to perform circumcision?**

2. **Why do you think we need a "sign?" Why such a physical one?**

---

[3] Although we are not certain when circumcision first started, we do know that it is very ancient in origin. Most scholars agree that it did not originate with the Jews. Thus, circumcision may have been a puberty initiation rite at one time, which the Jews adapted as a birth rite. The ceremony developed such symbolic significance for the Jewish people over the centuries that it became identified with them more so than any other group.

3. **Can you think of a reason that the "sign" is only expected of men, and not of women?**

What, according to the text, is the origin of the commandment for Jews to perform circumcision?

In the biblical context, circumcision was the covenantal obligation of the Israelites, in return for God's obligation to bring prosperity to the Jewish nation. The word "uncircumcised" came to be used metaphorically in the Bible for rebellious and stubborn people. Jeremiah says (9:25), "All the nations were uncircumcised in flesh, but all Israel were of uncircumcised heart."

We also find such a development in the *Siddur*. The *Shabbat Shacharit Amidah* states that "the uncircumcised do not enjoy the *Shabbat* rest."

וַיִּקַּח אַבְרָהָם אֶת־יִשְׁמָעֵאל בְּנוֹ וְאֵת כָּל־יְלִידֵי בֵיתוֹ וְאֵת כָּל־מִקְנַת
כַּסְפּוֹ כָּל־זָכָר בְּאַנְשֵׁי בֵּית אַבְרָהָם וַיָּמָל אֶת־בְּשַׂר עָרְלָתָם בְּעֶצֶם הַיּוֹם
הַזֶּה כַּאֲשֶׁר דִּבֶּר אִתּוֹ אֱלֹהִים: וְאַבְרָהָם בֶּן־תִּשְׁעִים וָתֵשַׁע
שָׁנָה בְּהִמֹּלוֹ בְּשַׂר עָרְלָתוֹ: וְיִשְׁמָעֵאל בְּנוֹ בֶּן־שְׁלֹשׁ עֶשְׂרֵה שָׁנָה בְּהִמֹּלוֹ
אֵת בְּשַׂר עָרְלָתוֹ: בְּעֶצֶם הַיּוֹם הַזֶּה נִמּוֹל אַבְרָהָם וְיִשְׁמָעֵאל בְּנוֹ:
וְכָל־אַנְשֵׁי בֵיתוֹ יְלִיד בָּיִת וּמִקְנַת־כֶּסֶף מֵאֵת בֶּן־נֵכָר נִמֹּלוּ אִתּוֹ:

Then Abraham took his son Ishmael, and all his homeborn slaves and all those he had bought, every male in Abraham's household, and he circumcised the flesh of their foreskins on that very day, as God had spoken to him. Abraham was ninety-nine years old when he circumcised the flesh of his foreskin, And his son Ishmael was thirteen years old when he was circumcised in the flesh of his foreskin. Thus Abraham and his son Ishmael were circumcised on that very day; And all his household, his homeborn slaves and those that had been bought from outsiders, were circumcised with him. (Bereishit 17:23-27)

1. **Most of us accept circumcision as something that is inherently Jewish. Why do you think this is so?**

2. **Circumcision is the only time Jews are told to make a permanent change to our bodies. If Judaism is so cautious about engaging in body piercing and tattooing, why do you think circumcision is encouraged?**

3. **Why only the "homeborn slaves," and not those who were born outside of Abraham's community? Is there a good reason for this difference?**

Judaism does not view circumcision as an idolatrous practice (which is one of the reasons tattooing and body piercing are frowned upon) or as a challenge to the concept of *b'tzelem Elohim* (made in the image of God). Rather, circumcision is a commandment from God that affirms our connection to God in each generation.

Do you agree with the rabbi's opinion on circumcision below? Why or why not?

There is a wonderful story in the Talmud about a Roman official who tried to outwit a rabbi by challenging him: "If God wanted you circumcised, why didn't God create you as God wanted?" Rabbi Oshaya answered confidently: "In order that man should perfect himself by fulfilling a Divine commandment." One might draw an analogy to Rabbi Oshaya's reply from some common modern ceremonies. The laying of the cornerstone of a building is left for dignitaries. Although they had no role in the physical activity of constructing the building, they symbolically complete the project. Similarly, the christening of a ship is a ceremonial honor left for one who did not hammer a single nail during the ship-building process, but who symbolically completes the task by propelling the ship on its first entry into the water. In our own tradition, we have such a custom. When a scribe makes a Torah scroll for a synagogue, he often leaves a few letters blank, having drawn only the outlines. The synagogue leaders fill in the blank letters, symbolizing their participation in the *mitzvah* of making a Torah. Thus the act of *brit milah* can be seen as our symbolic participation in the act of creation. We symbolically complete God's work.

When does the brit milah occur?

Typically, it is held eight days after the birth of a male child, even if that day is Yom Kippur or *Shabbat*. The ceremony takes precedence. In the event that medical need necessitates that the child remains in the hospital or is not considered hardy enough for the procedure, the *brit milah* must be delayed.

Brit Milah plays a prominent role throughout the Bible. Here is a sampling:

Ishmael, considered to be the father of Islam, was 13 when he was circumcised. The text below shows that the practice of *brit milah* had already been put in place by the time of Isaac's birth.

וַיָּמָל אַבְרָהָם אֶת־יִצְחָק בְּנוֹ בֶּן־שְׁמֹנַת יָמִים כַּאֲשֶׁר צִוָּה אֹתוֹ אֱלֹהִים:

And when his son Isaac was eight days old, Abraham circumcised him, as God had commanded him. (Bereishit 21:4)

Jacob's sons insisted that the men of Shechem become circumcised after their prince raped their sister Dinah. Later, when the townsmen were recovering from the surgery, Simon and Levi killed everyone.

אַךְ־בְּזֹאת נֵאוֹת לָכֶם אִם תִּהְיוּ כָמֹנוּ לְהִמֹּל לָכֶם כָּל־זָכָר: וְנָתַנּוּ
אֶת־בְּנֹתֵינוּ לָכֶם וְאֶת־בְּנֹתֵיכֶם נִקַּח־לָנוּ וְיָשַׁבְנוּ אִתְּכֶם וְהָיִינוּ לְעַם אֶחָד:
וְאִם־לֹא תִשְׁמְעוּ אֵלֵינוּ לְהִמּוֹל וְלָקַחְנוּ אֶת־בִּתֵּנוּ וְהָלָכְנוּ:

Only on this condition will we agree with you; that you will become like us in that every male among you is circumcised. Then we will give our daughters to you and take your daughters to ourselves; and we will dwell among you and become as one kindred. But if you will not listen to us and become circumcised, we will take our daughter and go. (Bereishit 34:15-17)

This is one of the more mysterious sections of the Bible. It appears that God tries to kill Moses because Moses did not circumcise his sons.

וַיְהִי בַדֶּרֶךְ בַּמָּלוֹן וַיִּפְגְּשֵׁהוּ יְהֹוָה וַיְבַקֵּשׁ
הֲמִיתוֹ: כה וַתִּקַּח צִפֹּרָה צֹר וַתִּכְרֹת אֶת־עָרְלַת בְּנָהּ וַתַּגַּע לְרַגְלָיו וַתֹּאמֶר

19

כִּי חֲתַן־דָּמִים אַתָּה לִי: וַיִּרֶף מִמֶּנּוּ אָז אָמְרָה חֲתַן דָּמִים לַמּוּלֹת:

At a night encampment on the way, the Lord encountered him and sought to kill him. So Zipporah took a flint and cut off her son's foreskin, and touched his legs with it, saying, You are truly a bridegroom of blood to me! And when God let him alone, she added, A bridegroom of blood because of the circumcision. (Shmot 4:24-26)

In this selection, circumcision dictates who can take part in Israelite ritual and who cannot.

וַיֹּאמֶר יְהוָֹה אֶל־מֹשֶׁה וְאַהֲרֹן זֹאת חֻקַּת
הַפָּסַח כָּל־בֶּן־נֵכָר לֹא־יֹאכַל בּוֹ: וְכָל־עֶבֶד אִישׁ מִקְנַת־כָּסֶף וּמַלְתָּה
אֹתוֹ אָז יֹאכַל בּוֹ: תּוֹשָׁב וְשָׂכִיר לֹא־יֹאכַל בּוֹ: בְּבַיִת אֶחָד יֵאָכֵל
לֹא־תוֹצִיא מִן־הַבַּיִת מִן־הַבָּשָׂר חוּצָה וְעֶצֶם לֹא תִשְׁבְּרוּ־בוֹ: כָּל־עֲדַת
יִשְׂרָאֵל יַעֲשׂוּ אֹתוֹ: וְכִי־יָגוּר אִתְּךָ גֵּר וְעָשָׂה פֶסַח לַיהוָֹה הִמּוֹל לוֹ
כָל־זָכָר וְאָז יִקְרַב לַעֲשֹׂתוֹ וְהָיָה כְּאֶזְרַח הָאָרֶץ וְכָל־עָרֵל לֹא־יֹאכַל בּוֹ:

The Lord said to Moses and Aaron: This is the law of the passover offering: No foreigner shall eat of it. But any slave a man has bought may eat of it once he has been circumcised. No bound or hired laborer shall eat of it. It shall be eaten in one house: you shall not take any of the flesh outside the house; nor shall you break a bone of it. The whole community of Israel shall offer it. If a stranger who dwells with you would offer the passover to the Lord, all his males must be circumcised; then he shall be admitted to offer it; he shall then be as a citizen of the country. But no uncircumcised person may eat of it. (Shmot 12:43-48)

Just after the Israelites cross the Jordan River, they are re-circumcised and the covenant renewed.

בָּעֵת הַהִיא אָמַר יְהוָֹה אֶל־יְהוֹשֻׁעַ עֲשֵׂה לְךָ חַרְבוֹת צֻרִים וְשׁוּב מֹל
אֶת־בְּנֵי־יִשְׂרָאֵל שֵׁנִית: וַיַּעַשׂ־לוֹ יְהוֹשֻׁעַ חַרְבוֹת צֻרִים וַיָּמָל אֶת־בְּנֵי
יִשְׂרָאֵל אֶל־גִּבְעַת הָעֲרָלוֹת: וְזֶה הַדָּבָר אֲשֶׁר־מָל יְהוֹשֻׁעַ כָּל־הָעָם הַיֹּצֵא
מִמִּצְרַיִם הַזְּכָרִים כֹּל | אַנְשֵׁי הַמִּלְחָמָה מֵתוּ בַמִּדְבָּר בַּדֶּרֶךְ בְּצֵאתָם
מִמִּצְרָיִם: כִּי־מֻלִים הָיוּ כָּל־הָעָם הַיֹּצְאִים וְכָל־הָעָם הַיִּלֹּדִים בַּמִּדְבָּר
בַּדֶּרֶךְ בְּצֵאתָם מִמִּצְרַיִם לֹא־מָלוּ: כִּי | אַרְבָּעִים שָׁנָה הָלְכוּ בְנֵי־יִשְׂרָאֵל
בַּמִּדְבָּר עַד־תֹּם כָּל־הַגּוֹי אַנְשֵׁי הַמִּלְחָמָה הַיֹּצְאִים מִמִּצְרַיִם אֲשֶׁר
לֹא־שָׁמְעוּ בְּקוֹל יְהוָֹה אֲשֶׁר נִשְׁבַּע יְהוָֹה לָהֶם לְבִלְתִּי הַרְאוֹתָם אֶת־הָאָרֶץ
אֲשֶׁר נִשְׁבַּע יְהוָֹה לַאֲבוֹתָם לָתֶת לָנוּ אֶרֶץ זָבַת חָלָב וּדְבָשׁ: וְאֶת־בְּנֵיהֶם
הֵקִים תַּחְתָּם אֹתָם מָל יְהוֹשֻׁעַ כִּי־עֲרֵלִים הָיוּ כִּי לֹא־מָלוּ אוֹתָם בַּדָּרֶךְ:
וַיְהִי כַּאֲשֶׁר־תַּמּוּ כָל־הַגּוֹי לְהִמּוֹל וַיֵּשְׁבוּ תַחְתָּם בַּמַּחֲנֶה עַד חֲיוֹתָם:

At that God said to Joshua: 'Make knives of flint, and circumcise again the children of Israel the second time.' And Joshua made him knives of flint, and circumcised the children of Israel at Gibeath-ha-araloth. And this is the cause why Joshua did circumcise: all the people that came forth out of Egypt, that were males, even all the men of war, died in the wilderness by the way, after they came forth out of Egypt. For all the people that came out were circumcised; but all the people that were born in the wilderness by the way as they came forth out of Egypt, had not been circumcised. For the children of Israel walked forty years in the wilderness, till all the nation, even the men of war that came forth out of Egypt, were consumed, because they hearkened not unto the voice of God; unto whom God swore that

God would not let them see the land which God swore unto their fathers that God would give us, a land flowing with milk and honey. And God raised up their children in their stead; them did Joshua circumcise; for they were uncircumcised, because they had not been circumcised by the way. And it came to pass, when all the nation were circumcised, every one of them, that they abode in their places in the camp, till they were whole. (Joshua 5:2-8)

The practice of *Brit Milah*, however, was often the subject of attacks by non-Jewish leaders. Antiochus, the villain of the Chanukah story, prohibited circumcision among the Jews, as did Hadrian, a Roman leader, some centuries later. Lack of circumcision became one of the distinguishing features of the early Christians (many of whom were Jews, originally).

Brit Milah was also neglected by Jews. At the time of the Maccabees (circa 2nd century BCE), there was a very high level of assimilation by Jews into the predominant Greek culture. Being circumcised, however, was seen as a liability. Unlike today where athletes compete in uniforms, Greek sporting events, as well as spas and other gathering places, included nude participants. Circumcision was seen as a mutilation of a body that was being celebrated in these events. Some Jews who desired to fit in better underwent surgical operations to cover up their circumcisions. Unfortunately for them, the surgeons of the day had not as yet perfected their procedures. Such Jews, as a result, became victims of even more derision, as it was evident to any onlooker that they had undergone such an operation.

MODERN OPPOSITION TO CIRCUMCISION

Modern times have also seen attacks on *Brit Milah*. Some claim that circumcision diminishes sexual pleasure. Others hold that it is akin to female genital mutilation, which involves the removal of the clitoris, that is practiced in some African countries. According to the American Academy of Pediatrics, the medical benefits of circumcision include fewer urinary tract infections and reduced risk of penile cancer. They do not, however, recommend routine circumcision of all baby boys.

Many people are squeamish about discussing *brit milah*, thinking that the procedure is very painful to the baby. According to the American Academy of Pediatrics, there is some evidence that newborns do feel pain. They recommend the use of several different methods to alleviating any pain felt by the newborn during circumcision. Many *mohalim* (plural of *mohel*) have adopted these practices.

WHO'S WHO?

Besides the guest of honor (the baby boy), several other people are involved in the *Brit Milah*. The ceremony is conducted by a person called a *mohel*. The *mohel* acts as an agent to the parents who hold the obligation to fulfill the *mitzvah* of *brit milah*. The *mohel* must meet certain minimum qualifications, both Judaically and medically. He or she must be well-versed in Jewish tradition, as well as personally observant. In addition, he must be properly trained and certified in the surgical procedures. Usually, this certification comes from a board consisting of rabbis, who can test the prospective *mohel* on all the laws of *brit milah*, and doctors, who can test surgical ability. The Conservative movement periodically offers training to become a *mohel*. It should be pointed out that the idea of a professional *mohel* is a compromise with human nature. The commandment of *brit milah* is an obligation of every father to circumcise his own son, based upon the biblical model provided by Abraham circumcising his own sons. Because, over the centuries, most fathers felt unable or unwilling of performing the act, the position of a community functionary developed. Thus, theoretically, any Jew can perform *brit milah*. In many traditional circles, the *mohalim* (plural for *mohel*) may not have modern medical credentials. This does not mean they are unqualified to practice. The truth of the matter is that some *mohalim* may be more qualified to perform circumcision than most doctors, because the *mohalim* are specialists in this area. However, because most Jews are unaware of this, they often demand either medical certification of some kind, or medical attendants present.

Look at your local Jewish paper. There is probably a section containing advertisements for *mohalim* Is it appropriate for *mohalim* to advertise their services? Should they be paid? What about rabbis who perform marriages or funerals?

The parents have an opportunity to choose people that they wan to honor for different roles within the *Brit Milah*. *These* roles are the *kvatter* (godfather), *kvatterin* (godmother) and *sandek*. In the ceremony, the "sandek" who is a person whose task it is to assist the *mohel*. This is considered a great honor and privilege, and is therefore usually assigned to one of the grandfathers. A *kvatterin* may take part in the ceremony by carrying the baby in to the room for the *brit milah*. This role is typically held by a grandmother or by the child's godmother. She would hand the baby to the *kvatter* who brings the baby fully into the room and hand's him off to the *mohel*. The *mohel* begins with a prayer and gives the baby to the *sandek*. Traditionally, the *sandek* held the child on his knees. Today, his participation is more symbolic than real, since the surgery is usually performed on a table, and then the baby is placed on the *sandek's* knees, whereas in the past, the entire operation took place with the child on the *sandek's* knees.

WHEN?

The *brit milah* must take place on the eighth day of the child's life. This means that if the baby was born on a Monday, then that *brit milah* will occur the following Monday, unless the baby was born after sunset on Monday and then the *brit milah* will occur on Tuesday (the Jewish day begins and ends at sunset). There is no apparent reason for this given in the Bible; it has simply been accepted. Having accepted this eight-day rule as binding, it applies <u>even</u> if the eighth day falls on *Shabbat* or *Yom Kippur*. Obviously, arrangements have to be made in advance to accommodate the *mohel* if the ceremony falls on one of these days.

The eighth-day rule is broken only for medical reasons. If there is any physical danger that might be incurred by the child if he were to undergo circumcision, the *brit milah* is postponed. Such a decision requires expert medical opinion. Our tradition dictates that if two previous children have died from causes attributed to circumcision, any subsequent child should not be circumcised until he is older and stronger (*Shulchan Aruch, Yoreh Deah*, 263:2). This is an example of the compassion for the individual and the flexibility inherent in *halachah* (Jewish law).

Finally, as a somber note, if a child dies before its eighth day of life, he must still be circumcised (*Shulchan Aruch, Yoreh Deah* 263:5). This stems from a folk tradition concerning the *Olam Haba* - the world to come. Even though the laws of mourning, about which we will learn later, dictate that a child who dies before the age of one month is not to be mourned, circumcision in a modified form must still take place in order to "qualify" the child for admittance to the *Olam Haba*.

WHERE?

There is no specific location for the *brit milah* to take place. Many families will have the *brit milah* in their home since this is most convenient for the mother and the child. Others may have it in the grandparents' home or at the synagogue. This decision is often based upon convenience and space.

Today, many hospitals automatically circumcise newborn males, since this practice has been widely accepted by the medical community as hygienic. A Jewish family, therefore, must assume the responsibility of informing the doctor or hospital officials not to do so. It should be stressed that the Jewish ceremony is more than just a surgical procedure.

SO, WHAT ACTUALLY HAPPENS?

First, the baby is typically carried into the room by the *kvaterin*. He is greeted by the guests, who proclaim:

בָּרוּךְ הַבָּא!

"Blessed is the one who comes."

The parents of the child then announce their willingness to conduct the *brit milah*:

I am ready to fulfill the mitzvah of having my son circumcised, as the praiseworthy Creator has commanded us in the Torah: "Throughout your generations, every male among you shall be circumcised when he is eight days old."

A second chair is also used during the *brit milah* although no one actually sits in it. The "Chair of Elijah" (הַכִּסֵּא שֶׁל אֵלִיָּהוּ) is a chair specifically set aside for circumcision. There are two explanations for Elijah's "participation" in this ceremony. During the period of Roman occupation of Palestine, many Jews were unwilling to practice *brit milah* because of the threat of persecution by the Romans if they did so. Elijah in heaven—as the story goes—complained to God about the Jews' breach of faith. God apparently had more patience with His people than did Elijah, and in order to teach Elijah this lesson, insisted that the prophet witness each *brit milah* from then on. The second explanation portrays Elijah in a more complimentary (and more traditional) light. According to this legend, Elijah will foretell the coming of the Messiah. Thus, he has always been identified with redemption and hope. His connection with the *brit milah* ceremony, then, is an expression of the collective hopes of the community for the newborn child—that he should "enter into the study of Torah, *hupah* (wedding canopy), and good deeds" (from the *Brit Milah* service). With this prayer, the community wishes for the child's own happiness and, through the child, the community's welfare. In this respect, Elijah has become the Jewish equivalent of a "guardian angel."

The child is briefly placed on the chair of Elijah and the *mohel,* will say a prayer asking for God to stand over them.

זֶה הַכִּסֵּא שֶׁל אֵלִיָּהוּ הַנָּבִיא זָכוּר לַטּוֹב.

This is the seat of Eliyahu Hanavi, Elijah the prophet, of blessed memory.

לִישׁוּעָתְךָ קִוִּיתִי יְיָ: שִׂבַּרְתִּי לִישׁוּעָתְךָ יְיָ, וּמִצְוֹתֶיךָ עָשִׂיתִי: אֵלִיָּהוּ
מַלְאַךְ הַבְּרִית, הִנֵּה שֶׁלְּךָ לְפָנֶיךָ, עֲמֹד עַל יְמִינִי וְסָמְכֵנִי. שִׂבַּרְתִּי
לִישׁוּעָתְךָ יְיָ. שָׂשׂ אָנֹכִי עַל אִמְרָתֶךָ, כְּמוֹצֵא שָׁלָל רָב: שָׁלוֹם רָב
לְאֹהֲבֵי תוֹרָתֶךָ, וְאֵין לָמוֹ מִכְשׁוֹל אַשְׁרֵי תִּבְחַר וּתְקָרֵב יִשְׁכֹּן
חֲצֵרֶיךָ, נִשְׂבְּעָה בְּטוֹב בֵּיתֶךָ קְדֹשׁ הֵיכָלֶךָ:

I wait for Your deliverance, Adonai. I hope for Your deliverance and I fulfill Your mitzvot. I hope for Your deliverance, Adonai. I rejoice over Your promise as one who finds great treasure. Great peace have they who love Your Torah; nothing makes them stumble. Happy is the one You choose to bring near, who will enjoy the goodness of Your house and the sanctity of Your temple. (Ber. 49:18, Tehillim 119:116, 162, 165; 65: 5a)

The *mohel* will then ask all those present to recite the following text:

נִשְׂבְּעָה בְּטוֹב בֵּיתֶךָ, קְדֹשׁ הֵיכָלֶךָ:

May we be filled with the blessings of Your house, Your holy Temple. (Teh. 65:5b)

The *mohel* will then place the baby on the *Sandek*'s knees who sits in a special chair or upon a table set up for the purpose of the circumcision. At this point, the *mohel* will ask the parents if they wish to perform the *brit milah* or if they authorize the *mohel* to perform it. This is done because as it was mentioned earlier, it is the parents' responsibility to perform the *brit milah*, but they may deputize someone to assist them. The *mohel* will then recite the following blessing:

בָּרוּךְ אַתָּה יְיָ אֱלֹהֵינוּ מֶלֶךְ הָעוֹלָם, אֲשֶׁר קִדְּשָׁנוּ בְּמִצְוֹתָיו וְצִוָּנוּ עַל
הַמִּילָה.

Praised are You, Adonai our God, who rules the universe, whose mitzvot add holiness to our lives and who gave us the mitzvah of circumcision.

THE OPERATION

It is at this point that the infant is circumcised.The operation of *brit milah* involves three stages: הֲתּוּךְ (*chituch*), פְּרִיעָה (*pri'ah*), and מְצִיצָה (*m'tzitzah*). In the first stage, the foreskin, which is simply a flap of skin covering the top of the penis (known as the glans), is pulled forward. While taut, a clamp is placed on this flap, resting against the glans. In this way, when the excess is cut off, there is no possibility of accidentally cutting into the penis itself.

After the foreskin is cut off (*chituch*), the second step, *pri'ah* (literally, uncovering), takes place. The part of the foreskin, and the mucous membrane under it, that had been held in the clamp, still cover a small part of the glans. This part is still attached to the penis. It is now peeled back, uncovering the entire glans. Eventually (within a few days) this peeled-back skin merges with the skin of the shaft of the penis, giving it a rim-like appearance.

The third step, *m'tzitzah* (literally, suction) involves drawing out the small amount of blood that forms when the excision is made. Nowadays, this is usually done by placing a glass tube containing a piece of cotton on the penis. The *mohel* sucks the tube, drawing the few drops of blood into it. In ancient times, this step was performed by placing the mouth directly on the penis; it was assumed that this was the best way to prevent infection. However, when medical science developed to the point where this procedure was viewed as likely to cause, rather than prevent, infection, this part of the procedure was adapted to the new knowledge. (This is not to say that the purpose of this is hygienic. It may be a fringe benefit, but the underlying reason for these specific steps is simply that tradition dictates it to be this way.)

After the circumcision, the father recites the following blessing:

בָּרוּךְ אַתָּה יְיָ אֱלֹהֵינוּ מֶלֶךְ הָעוֹלָם, אֲשֶׁר קִדְּשָׁנוּ
בְּמִצְוֹתָיו וְצִוָּנוּ לְהַכְנִיסוֹ בִּבְרִיתוֹ שֶׁל אַבְרָהָם אָבִינוּ.

Praised are You, Adonai our God, who rules the universe, whose mitzvot add holiness to our lives and who gave us the mitzvah to bring this child into the covenant of Abraham, our father.

Then, all those who are present at the ceremony will wish the child a life filled with Torah, marriage, and good deeds.

כְּשֵׁם שֶׁנִּכְנַס לַבְּרִית, כֵּן יִכָּנֵס לְתוֹרָה וּלְחֻפָּה וּלְמַעֲשִׂים
טוֹבִים. אָמֵן.

As he has entered the covenant, so may he enter the blessings of Torah, huppah, and a life of good deeds.

THE NAMING

Look ahead into the future when you have your first child.

1. What would you like to name your child?

2. Is your child named after someone special? Is it just a name that you happen to like? Does it have special meaning?

Following the *brit milah*, a blessing is recited over a cup of wine and the baby receives his Hebrew name. The following text formally names the child:

בָּרוּךְ אַתָּה יְיָ אֱלֹהֵינוּ מֶלֶךְ הָעוֹלָם, בּוֹרֵא פְּרִי הַגָּפֶן.
בָּרוּךְ אַתָּה יְיָ אֱלֹהֵינוּ מֶלֶךְ הָעוֹלָם, אֲשֶׁר קִדַּשׁ יָדִיד מִבֶּטֶן, וְחֹק
בִּשְׁאֵרוֹ שָׂם, וְצֶאֱצָאָיו חָתַם בְּאוֹת בְּרִית קֹדֶשׁ. עַל כֵּן בִּשְׂכַר זֹאת,
אֵל חַי חֶלְקֵנוּ צוּרֵנוּ צַוֵּה לְהַצִּיל יְדִידוּת שְׁאֵרֵנוּ מִשַּׁחַת, לְמַעַן
בְּרִיתוֹ אֲשֶׁר שָׂם בִּבְשָׂרֵנוּ. בָּרוּךְ אַתָּה יְיָ, כּוֹרֵת הַבְּרִית.

Praised are You, Adonai our God, who rules the universe, who sanctified our beloved patriarchs from the womb, who brings law and flesh together, sealing our offspring with the sign of the holy covenant. Therefore, living God, our Rock and our Portion, command good health for this child by virtue of Your covenant, so integral to our lives. Praised are You, Adonai, who establishes the covenant.

אֱלֹהֵינוּ וֵאלֹהֵי אֲבוֹתֵינוּ, קַיֵּם אֶת הַיֶּלֶד הַזֶּה לְאָבִיו וּלְאִמּוֹ, וְיִקָּרֵא
שְׁמוֹ בְּיִשְׂרָאֵל (פְּלוֹנִי בֶּן פְּלוֹנִי) יִשְׂמַח הָאָב בְּיוֹצֵא חֲלָצָיו וְתָגֵל
אִמּוֹ בִּפְרִי בִטְנָהּ, כַּכָּתוּב:
יִשְׂמַח אָבִיךָ וְאִמֶּךָ. וְתָגֵל יוֹלַדְתֶּךָ: וְנֶאֱמַר: וָאֶעֱבֹר עָלַיִךְ וָאֶרְאֵךְ
מִתְבּוֹסֶסֶת בְּדָמָיִךְ, וָאֹמַר לָךְ בְּדָמַיִךְ חֲיִי, וָאֹמַר לָךְ בְּדָמַיִךְ חֲיִי:
וְנֶאֱמַר: זָכַר לְעוֹלָם בְּרִיתוֹ, דָּבָר צִוָּה לְאֶלֶף דּוֹר: אֲשֶׁר כָּרַת אֶת
אַבְרָהָם וּשְׁבוּעָתוֹ לְיִשְׂחָק: וַיַּעֲמִידֶהָ לְיַעֲקֹב לְחֹק, לְיִשְׂרָאֵל בְּרִית
עוֹלָם: וְנֶאֱמַר: וַיָּמָל אַבְרָהָם אֶת יִצְחָק בְּנוֹ בֶּן שְׁמוֹנַת יָמִים, כַּאֲשֶׁר
צִוָּה אֹתוֹ אֱלֹהִים: הוֹדוּ לַיְיָ כִּי טוֹב, כִּי לְעוֹלָם חַסְדּוֹ: הַקָּהָל עוֹנֶה:
הוֹדוּ לַיְיָ כִּי טוֹב, כִּי לְעוֹלָם חַסְדּוֹ:(פְּלוֹנִי בֶּן פְּלוֹנִי) זֶה הַקָּטָן גָּדוֹל
יִהְיֶה, כְּשֵׁם שֶׁנִּכְנַס לַבְּרִית, כֵּן יִכָּנֵס לְתוֹרָה וּלְחֻפָּה וּלְמַעֲשִׂים
טוֹבִים. אָמֵן.

Our God and God of our ancestors, sustain this child. Let him be known among the people Israel as _____, son of _____ and _____. May his mother be blessed with regained strength and may both parents find joy in their child. With love and with wisdom may they be privileged to teach him the meaning of the covenant which he has entered today, and may they inspire him to seek the truth and the ways of peace. Through their example, may his heart be open to the Torah and its ways. May this child, (___first name only___), grow into greatness as a blessing to his family, to the Jewish people, and to all humanity. As he has entered the covenant, so may he attain the blessings of Torah, huppah, and good deeds. And let us say: Amen.

Then the parents and the *sandek* drink the wine.

May God bless you and keep you	יְבָרֶכְךָ יְיָ וְיִשְׁמְרֶךָ:
May God be with you and be gracious unto you.	יָאֵר יְיָ פָּנָיו אֵלֶיךָ וִיחֻנֶּךָּ:
May God show you kindness and give you peace.	יִשָּׂא יְיָ פָּנָיו אֵלֶיךָ וְיָשֵׂם לְךָ שָׁלוֹם:
	Bamidbar 6:24-26

The parents might recite the following:

The *brit milah*, like many other Jewish events, is not complete without food, despite the fact that the guest of honor will not be eating solids for a while. A *seudat mitzvah* (literally, a meal for a commandment. The festive meal that follow a ritual event, is served for the guests at the conclusion of the ceremony.

As part of the *Brit Milah* ceremony, we expressed the hope that our son, _____, would someday embrace Torah, establish a Jewish home, and illumine his life with *ma'asim tovim*, good deeds. In that spirit, we will be making a donation, in our son's name, to (a tzedakah program which com*Bat*s hunger) so that those who are truly hungry can also take part in this *se'udat mitzvah*.

For Discussion...

1. Our tradition has placed a great deal of emphasis on the importance of naming and names. Try this exercise: If you had a choice of a name for yourself, what name would you come up with?

2. Why does circumcision have to take place on the penis? If it is a symbolic act, why don't we just cut off a piece of the toe?

3. If someone approached you and said any of the following statements, how would you respond?
    The ceremony is *barbaric* butchery.
    The penis is being shortened by haphazardly cutting off part of it.
    The person performing the circumcision (*mohel*) is a witch doctor.

4. Why doesn't medical circumcision done automatically at birth in some hospitals satisfy the religious requirements of *brit milah*?

SIMCHAT BAT סדר שמחת בת

Unlike the *brit milah* ceremony for boys, there is no Biblical prescription that states how to celebrate the birth of a daughter or welcome the daughter into the covenant. In Ashkenazi communities, girls are usually named in the synagogue shortly after birth, but prior to about a month after birth. This involves calling the father and/or mother for an *aliyah* (being called to the Torah). A special blessing called a *misheberach* would be said that thanked God for God's kindness. Then, the daughter's name would be announced. In Sephardi communities, this ceremony is called a *zeved haBat* (gift of a daughter). Family and friends would gather at the baby's home.

The baby is then welcomed into the community with a short reading like this one from the Song of Songs:

יד יוֹנָתִי בְּחַגְוֵי הַסֶּלַע בְּסֵתֶר הַמַּדְרֵגָה הַרְאִינִי אֶת־מַרְאַיִךְ הַשְׁמִיעִינִי
אֶת־קוֹלֵךְ כִּי־קוֹלֵךְ עָרֵב וּמַרְאֵיךְ נָאוֶה:

O, my dove, in the cranny of the rocks, hidden by the cliff, let me see your face, let me hear your
voice, for your voice is sweet, your face is lovely. (Shir HaShirim, 2:14)

The baby is blessed and given a name.

In recent years, modern equivalents to *brit milah* for girls have evolved. They are called *Simhat Bat*, "the Rejoicing of a daughter" or *Brit B'not Yisrael*, "Covenant of the Daughters of Israel." One such attempt is included in this chapter. Some rituals for girls mirror the *brit milah* ceremony, while others are completely new.

How would you name a daughter?

27

Review the following ceremony for girls (*Brit B'not Yisrael*, or *Simhat Bat*). What concepts and elements are similar to the *Brit Milah*? Which are different?

The symbolism of Covenant has been integral to Jewish life and history. Traditionally, the boy has been linked with this Covenant through the act of naming and circumcision—*Brit Milah*. We now propose that girls also be welcomed into the Covenant of the Jewish people through the act of naming on *Shabbat*, since this day has served from biblical times as a covenantal symbol in Judaism. The ritual should take place before a community of family and friends in a ceremony which contains richness of symbolism and festivity. *Brit B'not Yisrael* is one such ceremony. It is suggested that it be performed in the home on the first *Shabbat* after the birth of the baby when the mother is capable of attending and participating. As much parental and family participation as possible is encouraged

This ceremony was written by Rabbis Sandy and Dennis Sasso, based upon a shorter version originally worked out together with Rebecca and Joel Alpert.

בְּרכה הַבָּא בשם יי!

"Blessed is she who comes in the name of God."

When Israel stood to receive the Torah, the Holy One, Blessed be He, said to them: I am giving you My torah. Present to Me good guarantors that you will guard it, and I shall give it to you.

They said: Our ancestors are our guarantors.

The Holy One, Blessed be He, said: Your ancestors are not sufficient guarantors. Yet bring Me good guarantors, and I shall give you the Torah.

They said: Master of the Universe, our prophets are our guarantors.

He said to them: The prophets are not sufficient guarantors. Yet bring Me good guarantors and I shall give you the Torah.

They said: Here, our children are our guarantors.

The Holy One, Blessed be He, said: They are certainly good guarantors. For their sake, I give the Torah to you.

(Song of Songs Rabbah 1, 24)

The parents continue:

We have been blessed with the gift of new life. We have shared love and pain and joy in bringing our daughter into life and have been privileged to participate in the marvel and beauty of creation.

By the way in which we live, we hope to teach our daughter to become a caring and loving person with a sense of her own worth and a respect for that of others. We dedicate ourselves to the creation of an exciting and meaningful Jewish home and to a life of compassion for others, hoping that our daughter will grow to cherish and emulate these ideals.

---

[4] Reprinted with permission from Moment Magazine, Volume 1, Number 1, May/June 1975, pp 50-51.

We gather together on this *Shabbat* with family and friends to bring our daughter into the Covenant of the Jewish people. For millennia the *Shabbat* has been a sign of covenantal commitment which has inspired generations of our people with the drive to creativity and the values of human dignity. Therefore, on this *Shabbat* (date of *Shabbat*) we bring our daughter before this community that she may be linked into the Covenant of the people of Israel.

בָּרוּךְ אַתָּה יְיָ אֱלֹהֵינוּ מֶלֶךְ הָעוֹלָם, אֲשֶׁר קִדְּשָׁנוּ
בְּמִצְוֹתָיו וְצִוָּנוּ לְהַכְנִיסוֹ אֶת בִּתֵּנוּ בִּבְרִית עַם יִשְׂרָאֵל.

Praised are You, Adonai our God, Who rules the universe, Whose mitzvot add holiness to our lives and who gave us the mitzvah to bring our daughter into the covenant of the people of Israel.

Every person born into this world represents something new, something that never existed before, something original and unique. It is the duty of every person in Israel to know and consider that she is unique in the world in her particular character and that there has never been someone like her in the world, for if there had been someone like her there would have been no need for her to be in the world. Every single person is a new thing in the world and is called upon to fulfill her particularity in the world. (Adapted from a passage by Martin Buber)

Uniqueness is concretized in the Jewish tradition through the act of naming. Therefore, we give this child the name _____ *Bat* (father's name) v' (mother's name).

קַיֵּם אֶת הַיַּלְדָּה הַזֹּאת לְאָבִיהָ וּלְאִמָּהּ וְיִקָּרֵא שְׁמָהּ בְּיִשְׂרָאֵל

_____ בַּת _____ וְ_____.

To be born also means to belong to the community, concretized in Judaism through Covenant.

As the *Shabbat* has been the sign of the Covenant for generations, so we bring _____ *Bat* _____ v' _____ into the Covenant of the people of Israel on (Hebrew date).

וְשָׁמְרוּ בְנֵי יִשְׂרָאֵל אֶת הַשַּׁבָּת, לַעֲשׂוֹת אֶת הַשַּׁבָּת לְדֹרֹתָם
בְּרִית עוֹלָם: בֵּינִי וּבֵין בְּנֵי יִשְׂרָאֵל אוֹת הִיא לְעוֹלָם, כִּי שֵׁשֶׁת יָמִים
עָשָׂה יְיָ אֶת הַשָּׁמַיִם וְאֶת הָאָרֶץ, וּבַיּוֹם הַשְּׁבִיעִי שָׁבַת וַיִּנָּפַשׁ.

The people of Israel shall keep the Shabbat, observing the Shabbat throughout the generations as a Covenant for all time; it shall be a sign for all time between Me and the people of Israel. For in six days did Adonai make the heavens and the earth, and on the seventh day, God ceased from work and rested. (Shmot 31: 16-17)

כְּשֵׁם שֶׁנִּכְנְסָה לַבְּרִית, כֵּן תִּכָּנֵס לְתוֹרָה וּלְחֻפָּה וּלְמַעֲשִׂים
טוֹבִים. אָמֵן.

As she has been brought into the Covenant of our people, so may she grow into a life of Torah, chupah, and good deeds.

On this day of our joy we raise this cup of wine in thankfulness for the fullness of life's blessing.

בָּרוּךְ אַתָּה יְיָ אֱלֹהֵינוּ מֶלֶךְ הָעוֹלָם, בּוֹרֵא פְּרִי הַגָּפֶן.

Blessed are you, Adonai our God, Ruler of the universe, who creates the fruit of the vine.

בָּרוּךְ אַתָּה יְיָ אֱלֹהֵינוּ מֶלֶךְ הָעוֹלָם, שֶׁהֶחֱיָנוּ וְקִיְּמָנוּ וְהִגִּיעָנוּ לַזְּמַן הַזֶּה.

Praised are You, Adonai our God, who rules the universe, for granting us life, for sustaining us, and for bringing us to this day.

(Parents drink the wine. A drop of wine should also be given to the child.)

May God bless you as God blessed Sarah, Rebecca, Rachel and Leah.

יְשִׂמֵךְ אֱלֹהִים כְּשָׂרָה רִבְקָה. רָחֵל וְלֵאָה

May God bless you and keep you

יְבָרֶכְךָ יְיָ וְיִשְׁמְרֶךָ:

May God be with you and be gracious unto you.

יָאֵר יְיָ פָּנָיו אֵלֶיךָ וִיחֻנֶּךָּ:

May God show you kindness and give you peace.

יִשָּׂא יְיָ פָּנָיו אֵלֶיךָ וְיָשֵׂם לְךָ שָׁלוֹם:

Questions to think about…

1. **In what way is this ritual meaningful?**

2. **What would you change or add to this ritual to make it more meaningful?**

3. **Has your family ever used such a ritual? If so, what was different?**

Group Activities

Divide into two groups—one which is pro-*Simchat Bat* and newer female-centered rituals, and one which is against this concept. Debate the following sentence: "Judaism should change to provide ritual outlets for females when they are not provided."
Each side should get a few minutes to prepare their arguments and presentations. In true debate format (pro point, con point, pro rebuttal, con rebuttal), let the two sides present their arguments.

Divide into groups of at least three people. Look at samples of *Simchat Bat* ceremonies as well as information about the notion of *Simchat Bat* and other similar rituals (this could include historical literature). Create your own *Simchat Bat* ceremony. Ceremonies may include song, poetry, artwork, etc.

Imagine not having a choice for your career. As the first-born child of your parents, your career has been chosen for you since the moment of your birth. Sounds strange, right? For some first-born Jewish males, this could be your fate if it weren't for a ceremony called *Pidyon HaBen*. Let's take a look at the sources for this unusual method of career choice.

וְהַעֲבַרְתָּ כָל־פֶּטֶר־רֶחֶם לַיהוָה וְכָל־פֶּטֶר | שֶׁגֶר בְּהֵמָה אֲשֶׁר יִהְיֶה לְךָ, הַזְּכָרִים לַיהוָה: וְכָל־פֶּטֶר חֲמֹר תִּפְדֶּה בְשֶׂה וְאִם־לֹא תִפְדֶּה וַעֲרַפְתּוֹ וְכֹל בְּכוֹר אָדָם בְּבָנֶיךָ תִּפְדֶּה: וְהָיָה כִּי־יִשְׁאָלְךָ בִנְךָ, מָחָר לֵאמֹר מַה־זֹּאת וְאָמַרְתָּ אֵלָיו בְּחֹזֶק יָד הוֹצִיאָנוּ יְהוָה מִמִּצְרַיִם מִבֵּית עֲבָדִים: וַיְהִי כִּי־הִקְשָׁה פַרְעֹה לְשַׁלְּחֵנוּ וַיַּהֲרֹג יְהוָה כָּל־בְּכוֹר בְּאֶרֶץ מִצְרַיִם מִבְּכֹר אָדָם וְעַד־בְּכוֹר בְּהֵמָה עַל־כֵּן אֲנִי זֹבֵחַ לַיהוָה כָּל־פֶּטֶר רֶחֶם הַזְּכָרִים וְכָל־בְּכוֹר בָּנַי אֶפְדֶּה:

You shall set apart for God every first issue of the womb: every male firstling that your cattle drop shall be the Lord's. But every firstling ass you shall redeem with a sheep; if you do not redeem it, you must break its neck. And you must redeem every first-born male among your children. And when, in time to come, your son asks you, saying, What does this mean? You shall say to him, It was with a mighty hand that God brought us out from Egypt, the house of bondage. When Pharaoh stubbornly refused to let us go, the Lord slew every first-born in the land of Egypt, the first-born of both man and beast. Therefore I sacrifice to God every first male issue of the womb, but redeem every first-born among my sons. (Shmot 13:12-15)

What do you think these texts mean when they say that a first-born son belongs to God?

What event is used as the reason for giving the first-born to God? What other traditions are tied to this event?

As you read through this source, two things become apparent. The source states the basic law that first-born sons "belong" to God. It also establishes a rationale for the law that the Israelite first-born are connected to the first-born Egyptians who were killed in the tenth plague. Because the first-born of Egypt died in order to save the Israelites (it was this last plague that finally convinced Pharaoh to release the Hebrews), the first-born of Israel owe a special gratitude to God. Therefore they are, in a sense, given to God by the parents. Historically, this was true. In the pre-slavery period, the first-born sons of the Israelite families were the leaders of their tribes and communities. This role included all religious leadership roles and duties, but as we see in this next source, this soon changed.

וַיֹּאמֶר מֹשֶׁה לְחֹתְנוֹ כִּי־יָבֹא אֵלַי הָעָם לִדְרֹשׁ אֱלֹהִים: כִּי־יִהְיֶה לָהֶם דָּבָר בָּא אֵלַי וְשָׁפַטְתִּי בֵּין אִישׁ וּבֵין רֵעֵהוּ וְהוֹדַעְתִּי אֶת־חֻקֵּי הָאֱלֹהִים וְאֶת־תּוֹרֹתָיו: וַיֹּאמֶר חֹתֵן מֹשֶׁה אֵלָיו לֹא־טוֹב הַדָּבָר אֲשֶׁר אַתָּה עֹשֶׂה:

The first issue of the womb of every being, man or beast, that is offered to the Lord, shall be yours; but you shall have the first-born of man redeemed, and you shall also have the firstling of unclean animals redeemed. Take as their redemption price, from the age of one month up, the money equivalent of five shekels by the sanctuary weight, which is twenty gerahs.[5] (Bamidbar 18:15-16)

Why do you think we are not given the option of continuing to offer our first-born to God, but are instead required to redeem first-born sons from God's service?

BINDING OF ISAAC

פרק כב א וַיְהִי אַחַר הַדְּבָרִים הָאֵלֶּה וְהָאֱלֹהִים נִסָּה אֶת־אַבְרָהָם וַיֹּאמֶר
אֵלָיו אַבְרָהָם וַיֹּאמֶר הִנֵּנִי: ב וַיֹּאמֶר קַח־נָא אֶת־בִּנְךָ אֶת־יְחִידְךָ
אֲשֶׁר־אָהַבְתָּ אֶת־יִצְחָק וְלֶךְ־לְךָ אֶל־אֶרֶץ הַמֹּרִיָּה וְהַעֲלֵהוּ שָׁם לְעֹלָה עַל
אַחַד הֶהָרִים אֲשֶׁר אֹמַר אֵלֶיךָ: ג וַיַּשְׁכֵּם אַבְרָהָם בַּבֹּקֶר וַיַּחֲבֹשׁ אֶת־חֲמֹרוֹ
וַיִּקַּח אֶת־שְׁנֵי נְעָרָיו אִתּוֹ וְאֵת יִצְחָק בְּנוֹ וַיְבַקַּע עֲצֵי עֹלָה וַיָּקָם וַיֵּלֶךְ
אֶל־הַמָּקוֹם אֲשֶׁר־אָמַר־לוֹ הָאֱלֹהִים: ד בַּיּוֹם הַשְּׁלִישִׁי וַיִּשָּׂא אַבְרָהָם
אֶת־עֵינָיו וַיַּרְא אֶת־הַמָּקוֹם מֵרָחֹק: ה וַיֹּאמֶר אַבְרָהָם אֶל־נְעָרָיו שְׁבוּ־לָכֶם
פֹּה עִם־הַחֲמוֹר וַאֲנִי וְהַנַּעַר נֵלְכָה עַד־כֹּה וְנִשְׁתַּחֲוֶה וְנָשׁוּבָה אֲלֵיכֶם:
ו וַיִּקַּח אַבְרָהָם אֶת־עֲצֵי הָעֹלָה וַיָּשֶׂם עַל־יִצְחָק בְּנוֹ וַיִּקַּח בְּיָדוֹ אֶת־הָאֵשׁ
וְאֶת־הַמַּאֲכֶלֶת וַיֵּלְכוּ שְׁנֵיהֶם יַחְדָּו: ז וַיֹּאמֶר יִצְחָק אֶל־אַבְרָהָם אָבִיו
וַיֹּאמֶר אָבִי וַיֹּאמֶר הִנֶּנִּי בְנִי וַיֹּאמֶר הִנֵּה הָאֵשׁ וְהָעֵצִים וְאַיֵּה הַשֶּׂה לְעֹלָה:
ח וַיֹּאמֶר אַבְרָהָם אֱלֹהִים יִרְאֶה־לּוֹ הַשֶּׂה לְעֹלָה בְּנִי וַיֵּלְכוּ שְׁנֵיהֶם יַחְדָּו:
ט וַיָּבֹאוּ אֶל־הַמָּקוֹם אֲשֶׁר אָמַר־לוֹ הָאֱלֹהִים וַיִּבֶן שָׁם אַבְרָהָם
אֶת־הַמִּזְבֵּחַ וַיַּעֲרֹךְ אֶת־הָעֵצִים וַיַּעֲקֹד אֶת־יִצְחָק בְּנוֹ וַיָּשֶׂם אֹתוֹ
עַל־הַמִּזְבֵּחַ מִמַּעַל לָעֵצִים: י וַיִּשְׁלַח אַבְרָהָם אֶת־יָדוֹ וַיִּקַּח אֶת־הַמַּאֲכֶלֶת
לִשְׁחֹט אֶת־בְּנוֹ: יא וַיִּקְרָא אֵלָיו מַלְאַךְ יְהוָה מִן־הַשָּׁמַיִם וַיֹּאמֶר אַבְרָהָם |
אַבְרָהָם וַיֹּאמֶר הִנֵּנִי: יב וַיֹּאמֶר אַל־תִּשְׁלַח יָדְךָ אֶל־הַנַּעַר וְאַל־תַּעַשׂ לוֹ
מְאוּמָה כִּי | עַתָּה יָדַעְתִּי כִּי־יְרֵא אֱלֹהִים אַתָּה וְלֹא חָשַׂכְתָּ אֶת־בִּנְךָ
אֶת־יְחִידְךָ מִמֶּנִּי: יג וַיִּשָּׂא אַבְרָהָם אֶת־עֵינָיו וַיַּרְא וְהִנֵּה־אַיִל אַחַר נֶאֱחַז
בַּסְּבַךְ בְּקַרְנָיו וַיֵּלֶךְ אַבְרָהָם וַיִּקַּח אֶת־הָאַיִל וַיַּעֲלֵהוּ לְעֹלָה תַּחַת בְּנוֹ:
יד וַיִּקְרָא אַבְרָהָם שֵׁם־הַמָּקוֹם הַהוּא יְהוָה | יִרְאֶה אֲשֶׁר יֵאָמֵר הַיּוֹם בְּהַר
יְהוָה יֵרָאֶה: טו וַיִּקְרָא מַלְאַךְ יְהוָה אֶל־אַבְרָהָם שֵׁנִית מִן־הַשָּׁמָיִם:
טז וַיֹּאמֶר בִּי נִשְׁבַּעְתִּי נְאֻם־יְהוָה כִּי יַעַן אֲשֶׁר עָשִׂיתָ אֶת־הַדָּבָר הַזֶּה וְלֹא
חָשַׂכְתָּ אֶת־בִּנְךָ אֶת־יְחִידֶךָ: יז כִּי־בָרֵךְ אֲבָרֶכְךָ וְהַרְבָּה אַרְבֶּה אֶת־זַרְעֲךָ
כְּכוֹכְבֵי הַשָּׁמַיִם וְכַחוֹל אֲשֶׁר עַל־שְׂפַת הַיָּם וְיִרַשׁ זַרְעֲךָ אֵת שַׁעַר אֹיְבָיו:
יח וְהִתְבָּרֲכוּ בְזַרְעֲךָ כֹּל גּוֹיֵי הָאָרֶץ עֵקֶב אֲשֶׁר שָׁמַעְתָּ בְּקֹלִי: יט וַיָּשָׁב
אַבְרָהָם אֶל־נְעָרָיו וַיָּקֻמוּ וַיֵּלְכוּ יַחְדָּו אֶל־בְּאֵר שָׁבַע וַיֵּשֶׁב אַבְרָהָם בִּבְאֵר
שָׁבַע:

1. And it came to pass after these things, that God tested Abraham, and said to him, Abraham; and he said, Behold, here I am. 2. And he said, Take now your son, your only son Isaac, whom you love, and go to the land of Moriah; and offer him there for a burnt offering upon one of the mountains which I will tell you. 3. And Abraham rose up early in the morning, and saddled his ass, and took

---

[5] A portion of a shekel which was a silver coin.

two of his young men with him, and Isaac his son, and broke the wood for the burnt offering, and rose up, and went to the place of which God had told him. 4. Then on the third day Abraham lifted up his eyes, and saw the place far away. 5. And Abraham said to his young men, Stay here with the ass; and I and the lad will go yonder and worship, and come back to you. 6. And Abraham took the wood of the burnt offering, and laid it upon Isaac his son; and he took the fire in his hand, and a knife; and they went both of them together. 7. And Isaac spoke to Abraham his father, and said, My father; and he said, Here am I, my son. And he said, Behold the fire and the wood; but where is the lamb for a burnt offering? 8. And Abraham said, My son, God will provide himself a lamb for a burnt offering; so they went both of them together. 9. And they came to the place which God had told him; and Abraham built an altar there, and laid the wood in order, and bound Isaac his son, and laid him on the altar upon the wood. 10. And Abraham stretched out his hand, and took the knife to slay his son. 11. And the angel of the Lord called to him from heaven, and said, Abraham, Abraham; and he said, Here am I. 12. And he said, Lay not your hand upon the lad, nor do anything to him; for now I know that you fear God, seeing that you did not withheld your son, your only son from me. 13. And Abraham lifted up his eyes, and looked, and behold behind him a ram caught in a thicket by his horns; and Abraham went and took the ram, and offered him up for a burnt offering in place of his son. 14. And Abraham called the name of that place Adonai-Yireh; as it is said to this day, In the Mount of the Lord it shall be seen. 15. And the angel of the Lord called to Abraham from heaven the second time, 16. And said, By myself have I sworn, said the Lord, for because you have done this thing, and have not withheld your son, your only son; 17. That in blessing I will bless you, and in multiplying I will multiply your seed as the stars of the heaven, and as the sand which is upon the sea shore; and your seed shall possess the gate of his enemies; 18. And in your seed shall all the nations of the earth be blessed; because you have obeyed my voice. 19. So Abraham returned to his young men, and they rose up and went together to Beersheba; and Abraham lived at Beersheba. (Bereishit 22: 1-20)

Think about the story of the Binding of Isaac. How is that connected to these texts?

This source shows us the way out of a life of servitude to God as a first-born. While wandering in the desert, the Jews constructed a central religious institution, the *Mishkan* (Tabernacle). One of the twelve tribes, *Levi*, was designated to perform ritual tasks in the *Mishkan* and assumed the religious and spiritual leadership. One family from the tribe, Aaron and his sons, was designated as *Kohanim* or Priests, and directed the *Mishkan*.

Thus, the responsibility of the spiritual leadership of the nation gradually passed from the first-born sons of every family to the *Kohanim* and Levi'im (or Levites). The *Pidyon Ha'ben* ceremony, in one sense, symbolizes the transfer of authority. Since the first-born were originally charged with the responsibility of God's work, they had to be returned to their families once this duty was taken over by the Priests. That is why the *Pidyon Ha'ben* is a "redemption" of the first-born. The parent buys his son back from God through God's appointed leaders, the *Kohanim*.

On a second level, we can see still another factor behind this ancient life cycle ceremony. We know that the people that became the first Hebrews grew up under the influence of Canaanite civilization. The Canaanites sacrificed their first-born sons to the gods as a matter of religious obligation. The Bible gives us a hint of this in the story of the sacrifice of Isaac. One way to understand the story is to see it as representative of the revolutionary character of Abraham and the then new Jewish religion. Abraham, as a citizen of Canaan, prepared to do what all Canaanite fathers did—to offer his first-born son on an altar to God. (Although Ishmael was older than Isaac, the latter was considered the first-born from a legal standpoint, because of his birth to Sarah, whereas Ishmael's mother, Hagar, was—as a concubine—of lower rank.) But Abraham came to realize that the God, in whom he believed, the God that created the world, must have wanted his creatures to live. And so, in a radical break with the traditions of his environment, Abraham did not go ahead with the sacrifice of his beloved son.

Whatever interpretation of this story one accepts, the fact is that after all, the slaughter of Isaac did not take place. Many of the traditional commentaries indicate their interpretation that God never intended to allow Abraham actually to go through with it. Whether it was the guiding hand of God, or the independent decision of Abraham, child sacrifice became taboo for Jews. Perhaps the ancient Hebrews wanted to demonstrate their disgust with the Canaanite culture by developing a ceremony that represented their conception of God's true relationship to man.

We offer our first-born to God out of gratitude and humility. We believe that the laws of nature which dictate the workings of reproduction, and thus the creation of life, are written by God. Therefore, we realize that as partners with God in creation, the child belongs partly to God also. But God wants us to enjoy the fruits of our labor and to sanctify the world in which we live. For this reason, God allows us to "redeem" our first-born from God by "buying" him back.

RULES OF *PIDYON* HA BEN

The ceremony depends on the mother; it must be her first-born. Therefore if the child is the first-born son of a second wife, *Pidyon Ha'ben* must take place, even though the father may have already redeemed a son through his first wife.

Not every first-born male, though, needs to have a *Pidyon HaBen*. First, if either parent is a *Kohen* or *Levi*, the child need not be redeemed. *Pidyon Ha'ben* does not take place if the child is born by caesarean section, because of the verse which states: "the first issue of the womb." In other words, if birth takes place outside the womb, then child need not be redeemed. Similarly, if a previous pregnancy ended in a miscarriage, the next child to be born, even if it is first to live, is not redeemed—again, because it is not the first issue of the womb. It is thus the combination of two factors—being the first-born and being born of the womb—that is the requirement for *Pidyon Ha'ben*.

Unlike *brit milah*, if the day on which the *Pidyon Ha'ben* is to take place (the 31st day of life) is a *Shabbat* or *Yom Tov*, the ceremony is postponed until the next day. This is due to the interpretation of the verses in the Bible which dictate the two rituals. The verse for *brit milah* states:

וּבַיּוֹם הַשְּׁמִינִי יִמּוֹל בְּשַׂר עָרְלָתוֹ:

On the eight day the flesh of his foreskin shall be circumcised (Vayikra 12:3).

That verse gives a definite date, while the verse mentioning *Pidyon Ha'ben* states:

וּפְדוּיָו מִבֶּן־חֹדֶשׁ תִּפְדֶּה בְּעֶרְכְּךָ כֶּסֶף חֲמֵשֶׁת שְׁקָלִים בְּשֶׁקֶל הַקֹּדֶשׁ עֶשְׂרִים גֵּרָה הוּא:

Take as their redemption price from the age of one month up, the money equivalent of five shekels by the sanctuary weight, which is twenty gerahs. (Bamidbar 18:16).

Since this is somewhat vague, the Rabbis assumed that *Shabbat* and *Yom Tov* superseded the *Pidyon Ha'ben*.

After a brief introductory statement by the rabbi, the parents, with their son resting on a pillow, stand before the *Kohen* and announce that this is their first-born son.

This is our firstborn son, the first issue of his mother. The *Kadosh Barukh Hu* has commanded us to redeem him, as it is stated:

וּפְדוּיָו מִבֶּן־חֹדֶשׁ תִּפְדֶּה בְּעֶרְכְּךָ כֶּסֶף חֲמֵשֶׁת שְׁקָלִים בְּשֶׁקֶל הַקֹּדֶשׁ עֶשְׂרִים גֵּרָה הוּא:

"Take as (the firstborn's) redemption price, from the age of one month up, the money equivalent of five shekalim by the sanctuary weight, which is twenty gerahs" (Bamidbar 18:16)

And it is further written:

קַדֶּשׁ־לִי כָל־בְּכוֹר פֶּטֶר כָּל־רֶחֶם בִּבְנֵי יִשְׂרָאֵל בָּאָדָם וּבַבְּהֵמָה לִי הוּא:

"Consecrate to Me every firstborn, man and beast, the first issue of every womb among the Israelites is Mine" (Shmot 13:2)

The *Kohen* then asks the parents if they wish to dedicate their son in service of the *Kohanim* or redeem him:

מַאי בָּעִית טְפֵי, לִיתֵּן לִי בִּנְךָ בְּכוֹרְךָ שֶׁהוּא פֶּטֶר רֶחֶם לְאִמּוֹ, אוֹ בָּעִית לְפִדוֹתוֹ בְּעַד חָמֵשׁ סְלָעִים כִּדְמְחַיְּבַתָּא מִדְּאוֹרַיְתָא.

What is your preference: to give me your firstborn son, the first issue of his mother, or to redeem him for five shekalim as you are obligated, according to the Torah?

Then, the parents state their intent to redeem their son.

חָפֵץ אֲנִי לִפְדוֹת אֶת בְּנִי, וְהֵא-לָךְ דְּמֵי פִדְיוֹנוֹ כִּדְמְחַיְּבַתִּי מִדְּאוֹרַיְתָא.

We wish to redeem our son. We present you with the cost of his redemption as required by the Torah.

The redemption involves the exchange of five shekels, or their equivalent, as mandated by the Bible. Today, it is customary to use five silver dollars. Coins should be used, rather than paper money, because the mode of exchange must have inherent value, and paper money has only symbolic value. Usually, the *Kohen* returns the money to the father or gives it to *Tzedakah*.

The parents will place the coins on the pillow and recite the following blessings:

בָּרוּךְ אַתָּה יְיָ אֱלֹהֵינוּ מֶלֶךְ הָעוֹלָם, אֲשֶׁר קִדְּשָׁנוּ בְּמִצְוֹתָיו וְצִוָּנוּ עַל פִּדְיוֹן הַבֵּן.

Praised are You, Adonai our God, who rules the universe, whose mitzvot add holiness to our lives and who gave us the mitzvah of the firstborn son's redemption.

בָּרוּךְ אַתָּה יְיָ אֱלֹהֵינוּ מֶלֶךְ הָעוֹלָם, שֶׁהֶחֱיָנוּ וְקִיְּמָנוּ וְהִגִּיעָנוּ לַזְּמַן הַזֶּה.

Praised are You, Adonai our God, who rules the universe, for granting us life, for sustaining us, and for bringing us to this day.

Then the *Kohen* takes the coins and holds them over the baby's head. He then finalizes the transaction and the ceremony concludes with the *Kohen* reciting the Priestly blessing over the child.

יְשִׂמְךָ אֱלֹהִים כְּאֶפְרַיִם וְכִמְנַשֶּׁה.

יְבָרֶכְךָ יְיָ וְיִשְׁמְרֶךָ: יָאֵר יְיָ פָּנָיו אֵלֶיךָ וִיחֻנֶּךָּ: יִשָּׂא יְיָ פָּנָיו אֵלֶיךָ וְיָשֵׂם לְךָ שָׁלוֹם:

כִּי אֹרֶךְ יָמִים וּשְׁנוֹת חַיִּים וְשָׁלוֹם יוֹסִיפוּ לָךְ:

יְיָ שֹׁמְרֶךָ יְיָ צִלְּךָ עַל יַד יְמִינֶךָ:

יְיָ יִשְׁמָרְךָ מִכָּל רָע, יִשְׁמֹר אֶת נַפְשֶׁךָ:

כִּי אֹרֶךְ יָמִים וּשְׁנוֹת חַיִּים וְשָׁלוֹם יוֹסִיפוּ לָךְ:

Through this exchange your son is redeemed. May this child enjoy a life of Torah and godliness. As he has attained redemption, so may he attain the blessings of Torah, hupah, and a life of good deeds. And let us say: Amen.

What is the role of the first-born in your family (if it is not you...)

What is your role? Is it different from your siblings?

If you are an only child, has your role been different from that of your friends? In what way?

For Discussion...

1. Looking at your own family structure can you tell if the first-born child has a different set of responsibilities from other brothers and sisters?

2. Give examples of how the Bible demonstrates special significance of the first-born child.

3. Now show how the Bible tempers this outlook by seeming to go out of its way to indicate that a first-born son is not necessarily the wisest and the most deserving of honor or power.

4. In recent years, a new ceremony has evolved for first-born girls. It has been given a variety of names, e.g. *Pidyon HaBat* ("redemption of the daughter"), *seder kidushat chaye hamishpacha* ("order of the sanctification of family life"), or *Kiddush peter rechem* ("sanctification of the one who opens the womb"). How do you feel about altering the *Pidyon HaBen* ritual to include girls? What should such a ritual encompass?

In 1993, the Committee on Jewish Law and Standards considered a paper written by Rabbi Gerald Skolnik on whether or not there should be a ceremony for first-born female children. Rabbi Skolnik concluded, and the committee approved, that the Biblically mandated practice of *Pidyon* HaBen is restricted to male first-born children, and should not be expanded to include first-born female children. However, all gatherings which serve the purpose of enhancing the sense of blessing and specialness associated with the birth of a first-born female child are to be encouraged.

> While the desire to enhance the sense of worth and value to the Jewish community of a female child is understandable and laudable, it would be preferable to include the element of *Bat B'racha* as a component of a *Simchat Bat* ceremony, rather than create a new ceremony which few would be likely to utilize and which would have no true *halakhic* integrity.

> The general question of whether or not a *Pidyon Haben* ceremony might properly be performed for a female first-born child is answered clearly and unequivocally in the Torah. The mandated practice of redeeming the first-born son from his special religious obligations via the agency of the *Levi'im* (or today their decendents, the *kohanim*; see Exod. 13:1-2, and Num. 3:11-13 and 18:15-16) clearly holds only with regard to male first-born children, and not female. No matter what the motivation, one cannot change history and retroactively project this obligation onto a female child.

The absence of a parallel ceremony for girls stems from two primary rationales: 1- the *Pidyon* haben ceremony is widely unused either because of unfamiliarity with the ceremony, or because of abortions or miscarriages of the first pregnancy which would make the ceremony unnecessary. 2- The Torah specifically states that it is mandated for first-born sons and does not give a base upon which to extend the mandate to females.

> To a great degree, the development and increasing prevalence of *Simchat Bat* ceremonies has effectively served the purpose of providing a meaningful and parallel yet unique vehicle for welcoming a female child into the covenant between Israel and God. The task before me, therefore, was not to create some sort of ritual expressing the covenant idea. And, through the true thematic rationale for the ceremony would be redemption, it also increasingly seemed to be a mistake to create a ceremony which would assume that woman needed to be redeemed from obligations which they never had in the first place.

Rabbi Skolnik concluded by suggesting that the aspect of "first-born-ness" should be celebrated in the *Simchat Bat*, rather than creating an entirely new ceremony. The absence of the time-mandate for this ceremony (as opposed to the *brit milah* which takes place on the eighth day), allows parents the opportunity to hold the *Simchat Bat* at their convenience— including the option of holding it on the same day that the *Pidyon* HaBen would have been held for a male first-born child. A further suggestion was added to thematically and appropriately connect the notion of a *Pidyon* ceremony into the *Simchat Bat* ceremony by Rabbi Laurence Sebert.

> The juxtaposition of the commandment to redeem the first-born Israelite child in *Shmot* 13 with the account of the plague of the slaying of the Eqyptian first-born in *Shmot* 12 has, to some commentators, suggested an association between the two. In that light, the well-known text from *Sh'mot Rabbah* 1:12 seems particularly appropriate:

דרש רבי עקיבה בשכר נשים צדקניות שבאותו הדור נגאלו אבותינו ממצרים.

Rabbi Akiva interpreted: By virtue of the reward due the righteous women of the generation of the Shmot were our forefathers redeemed from Egypt.

What better or more appropriate connecting text could there be?

CONVERSION AND ADOPTION

The general attitude of Judaism towards adoption is summed up in the quote from *Shmot* Rabbah (46:5) below:

"The one who raises a child, and not the one who merely begot him, is the one who is called father or mother."

This is not to negate the rights of birth parents, but rather to encourage the full integration of adopted children into Jewish society.

If the child is Jewish by birth (according to halacha, this means that the child's mother is Jewish) then no conversion is necessary. Non-Jewish children, however, are required to convert. This is done by immersing the child in a *mikvah* (ritual *Bat*h). Boys are required to undergo a covenant ceremony, i.e. a *brit milah* (the parents may opt to have a *simcha Bat* for a girl, but it is not required). For those children that are converted, it is considered appropriate to discuss the conversion and whether they want to remain Jewish at the time of the *bar/Bat mitzvah* since the conversion was done prior to their ability to comprehend.

For a male baby, performing the *brit milah* is rather simple. For an older child or an adult convert, the decision becomes more complicated. Conversion is a serious event, and the Jewish attitude is to discourage adult converts as much as possible, on the assumption that one may desire to convert for a variety of reasons, without realizing the obligations of being a Jew. If the individual still desires to convert after knowing what is involved, and after comprehending the process of *brit milah*, then we embrace him with open arms, on the confident assumption that the individual is converting out of total sincerity. In the event that the convert has been surgically circumcised at birth (the same is true for a Jewish child medically—but not religiously—circumcised in the hospital), a simple procedure called *Hatafat Dam* (literally, the drawing of a drop of blood) takes place. As the name indicates, a mere drop of blood is drawn from the glans of the penis by sticking it with a pin, while the prayers and benedictions of the regular *brit milah* ceremony are recited. The child would then need to be immersed in a kosher *mikvah*.

LOOKING AHEAD

Look ahead to eventually being a parent:

What are you scared of?

What are you excited about?

Do you want to eventually be a parent? Why or why not?

What would you do differently from your own parents? What would you do the same?

Wednesday- Day #1—I am here- yippee!! From the hospital my parents called everyone. The first person they called was a *Mohel.* They told me that he was someone who performed a *brit milah* (circumcision) on Jewish baby boys when they are eight days old. This person, whether it is a man or a woman, is not necessarily a doctor but is trained in what they do. They did not tell me what a circumcision is. I will have to wait and see. They told the *Mohel* that I was healthy, so that means I could have the *brit milah* on the eighth day which would be next Wednesday since I was born before sun down I began to count down.

Thursday- Day #2—I am still in the hospital but I am going to be going home in a couple of hours. Boy it's hot in the nursery. Once we get home, lots of people come to visit me. They all coo and aah. How silly. Some of my parents' friends come and they talk about a party after the *brit milah.* They say it's a called a *seudat mitzvah.* That seems to be a special meal after the ceremony. The friends say that they will help my parents by making all the food. Yummy. I hope I get to taste some of it. This formula stuff is already getting a bit boring. Everyone is told about the *brit milah.* Lots of people are coming. But what is it??

Friday- Day #3—It's my first *Shabbat* in the world and my parents are very excited. They put up a poster in the synagogue inviting everyone back to our home after services. They told everyone it is called a *shalom zachar.* That's when you welcome a baby boy or girl into the world for their first *Shabbat.* We lit candles and *Ima* and *Aba* had friends over for dinner. Why was everyone's eyes getting so watery? What is the big deal?

Shabbat- Day #4—We all went to the synagogue. There is lots of singing there. Lots of people came over to say *Shabbat* shalom.

Sunday- Day #5—*Ima* and *Aba* were alone for the first time since I was born. They were talking about my name. They have not told anyone what my name is. That is another thing that is done at the *brit milah. Ima* says my name is very important because it will tell people who I am. She keeps talking about "Jewish identity" and that is why I am getting a Hebrew name. I am not sure what "identity" is. *Aba* says that I am named after two grandpas who are no longer living but whom *Ima* and *Aba* loved very much. Everyone else keeps calling me "baby boy Brodie." What a funny name!!

Monday- Day #6—*Ima* and *Aba* seem a bit tense today. They are talking about who will do what job at the *brit milah.* There are so many jobs that have to be done. They wrote a list and I got a peek at it-

1. *kvaterim* (These are like godparents) They are going to carry me into the synagogue. (Where will my Ima and Aba be I wonder?)

2. Handing the baby to the *mohel* to sit on the chair of Elijah. These are *Ima* and *Aba's* friends.

3. *Sandek/sandeket.* This is the person who will hold me during the actual *brit milah. Ima* and *Aba* discuss this a lot. This has to be someone special.

4. *Kiddush* and naming. This is the person who will say *kiddush* and then will name me. That is going to be a rabbi friend of my parents'. People keep coming over to visit me. I like all this attention!!

---

[6] Excerpted from "Look Who's Talking" by Rabbi Amanda Brodie, Kol Kadima, 1997

Tuesday Day #7—Boy is it crazy at our house today! People keep coming over with big bags and they are staying with us. What is all this fuss about? *Ima* and *Aba* talk quietly in one room and they decide who the *sandeket* is going to be. It's going to be Shira! I like her, she gave me a *Bath* today.

Wednesday Day #8—The big day has arrived! *Ima* and *Aba* seem very nervous. Can't think why. *Aba* has decided that the *mohel* will perform the circumcision, although he could have done it himself, since Jewish fathers are commanded to do this in the Torah. *Aba* said that he was too nervous, even though in the Torah Abraham circumcised Isaac himself. *Aba* said he does not have such a steady hand.

Ima and *Aba* take me to the synagogue and hand me to the *kvaterim* who hand me to the people who are going to sit me in the chair of Elijah.

Then the *mohel* takes me and sits me on Shira's lap for the big moment. I don't like the fact that the *mohel* holds me very tightly and then he takes my diaper off. What is going on? The *mohel* says some blessings in Hebrew. These blessings welcome me into the Covenant of the Jewish people. That means I have to behave like a Jewish boy and that also means that I am now part of the people of Israel. Then the *mohel* cuts off the foreskin of my penis. This like a sign that I am a Jewish kid. It hurts a bit but then the *mohel* lets me suck on a piece of cloth soaked in wine and that is yummy so I don't feel so bad after all. While I am enjoying the wine, Hilda holds me and Rabbi Gail says *Kiddush* and gives me my name. I am called Yonatan Lev Brodie. Cool name, don't you think?

Just before we leave the *Bimah*, another rabbi comes to talk about the Torah. He is interesting but it is time for a nap so I don't pay too much attention. Then two more people take me out of the synagogue to my *Ima's* cozy arms. *Layla Tov.*

bar/ bat mitzvah

More than any other Jewish activity, the *Bar* or *Bat Mitzvah* seems to be the quintessential North American Jewish experience. Countless jokes have been made about the requisite speech given by the *Bar/Bat Mitzvah* or about the child's voice suddenly cracking. The experience has been portrayed in movies, such as *Keeping the Faith*, as something that most Jewish thirteen-year-olds experience. We are told that when we turn 12 for girls or 13 for boys, we become Jewish adults.

1. **In what way were you treated differently after your *Bar/Bat Mitzvah*?**

2. **Did you feel like an "adult?" Why or why not?**

3. **If you did not feel much like an adult, when do you think you will be an "adult?"**

How Was My Bar or Bat Mitzvah…

A Cause For Rejoicing	Something that tied me to tradition	Something that made me feel important	Something that helps Jewish unity

Although my father is the cantor of my synagogue, I had grown up in a small town and never had the chance to learn about the Bar Mitzvah experience. When it came time for me to start my preparations, I had almost no idea what my Bar Mitzvah was actually supposed to be like. Would I look different? Would I be taller? Before I knew it, November 16 came up. As I came up to the bimah *to lead services, I looked around at the whole congregation. They were waiting for me. I understood right at that moment that a Bar Mitzvah wasn't about gifts, or becoming taller. It was about becoming a member of the Jewish community. The thought excited me. I was now a part of the group.*

With all the hype that goes into a person's Bar Mitzvah, one doesn't usually think about its true meaning. I would encourage everyone to slow down for a moment and think about it. It only happens once.[7]

Based upon its place in North American Jewish culture, one would think that the *Bar/Bat Mitzvah* has a long history as a life-cycle event for Jews and would appear in our most sacred texts. However, there is no reference to it in the Bible at all. In fact, turning thirteen does not show up as a significant age for anything; rather a different age is cited:

כֹּל הָעֹבֵר עַל־הַפְּקֻדִים מִבֶּן עֶשְׂרִים שָׁנָה וָמַעְלָה יִתֵּן תְּרוּמַת יְהֹוָה:

Everyone who is entered in the records, from the age of twenty years up, shall give the Lord's offering. (Shmot 30:14)

מִבֶּן עֶשְׂרִים שָׁנָה וָמַעְלָה כָּל־יֹצֵא צָבָא בְּיִשְׂרָאֵל תִּפְקְדוּ אֹתָם לְצִבְאֹתָם אַתָּה וְאַהֲרֹן:

You and Aaron shall record them by their groups, from the age of twenty years up, all those in Israel who are able to bear arms. (Bamidbar 1:3)

In these texts, we learn that only those over 20 will be counted in the census and can serve in the military. So where does the concept of becoming a Jewish man or woman at 13 come from?

One possibility is that it comes from this text about Jacob and Esau:

10. AND THE BOYS GREW (XXV, 27). R. Phinehas said in R. Levi's name: They were like a myrtle and a wild rose-bush growing side by side; when they attained to maturity, one yielded its fragrance and the other its thorns. So for thirteen years both went to school and came home from school. After this age, one went to the house of study and the other to idolatrous shrines. R. Eleazar b. R. Simeon said: A man is responsible for his son until the age of thirteen; thereafter he must say, ' Blessed is He who has now freed me from the responsibility of this boy.' (Bereishit Rabbah 63:10)

As this source indicates, the children are changing and making adult decisions. The twins, Jacob and Esau, cease to be reflections of each other and went their separate ways. Each of the decisions made at this age is about rejecting or accepting a structure of belief in God and behavior. Perhaps this is why the rabbis chose thirteen as the transition point to adulthood.

---

[7] By Jay Rapaport, excerpted from Kol Kadima, Summer 1997.

Another possibility is found in *Pirke Avot* (5:21), where it states that:

הוּא הָיָה אוֹמֵר, בֶּן חָמֵשׁ שָׁנִים לַמִּקְרָא, בֶּן עֶשֶׂר לַמִּשְׁנָה, בֶּן שְׁלֹשׁ עֶשְׂרֵה לַמִּצְוֹת, בֶּן חֲמֵשׁ עֶשְׂרֵה לַתַּלְמוּד, בֶּן שְׁמוֹנֶה עֶשְׂרֵה לַחֻפָּה, בֶּן עֶשְׂרִים לִרְדּוֹף, בֶּן שְׁלֹשִׁים לַכֹּחַ, בֶּן אַרְבָּעִים לַבִּינָה, בֶּן חֲמִשִּׁים לָעֵצָה, בֶּן שִׁשִּׁים לַזִּקְנָה, בֶּן שִׁבְעִים לַשֵּׂיבָה, בֶּן שְׁמוֹנִים לַגְּבוּרָה, בֶּן תִּשְׁעִים לָשׁוּחַ, בֶּן מֵאָה כְּאִלּוּ מֵת וְעָבַר וּבָטֵל מִן הָעוֹלָם:

He (Yehudah ben Tema) used to say: At the age of five, (one is ripe) for Bible; at ten, for Mishnah, at thirteen, for mitzvot; at fifteen, for Talmud; at eighteen for the marriage canopy; at twenty, for pursuit; at thirty, for vigor: at forty, for understanding; at fifty, for counsel; at sixty, to be an elder; at seventy, for gray hair; at eighty, for strength; at ninety, to bend over; at one hundred, as if he had died and passed away and disappeared from the world.

There is a clear developmental progression indicated by this source. Formal schooling begins at age 5 similar to the way we start kindergarten at 5. After several years of basic studies, one moves on to the *Mishnah* which is an early Rabbinic explanation of Jewish law. Then, at age 13, after one has received a strong foundation, one begins to perform the *mitzvot* (commandments).

From this statement, we see that the fulfillment of the *mitzvot* follows the study of them. A child under the age of thirteen is not expected to be able to apply his textual knowledge to abstract conceptual matters, which would be necessary for having a rationale for fulfilling the commandments. That being the case, we do not hold a child responsible for his actions that violate Jewish law. Once the child reaches thirteen, however, the consequences for all of his actions are upon his own head. After thirteen, the child is no longer considered a minor and can, therefore, serve as a witness for legal documents and be counted in a *minyan*, as well as be expected to perform all requirements incumbent on a Jewish male, such as wearing *tefillin* every morning. A quick look at human development begins to show us that matters of legal status were connected to physical maturity. Thirteen is the age when many of the more obvious signs of puberty begin to emerge in a boy, while in girls who mature earlier these signs appear at about age 12. The rabbis must have been aware of this as there are several other sources which point to the importance of age 13 for boys.

Questions to think about…

1. **In what way is the *Bar/Bat Mitzvah* meaningful?**

2. **What would you add to this ritual to make it more meaningful?**

3. **What does your family already add to this ritual?**

Almost every culture in the world has some kind of initiation rites that herald a child's entrance into puberty, For some, this stage in life is marked by circumcision (for example, among the Muslims). For others, it may involve the requirement to pass some physical test demonstrating the child's physical prowess (for example, among some Native American tribes). One can imagine that a child in such circumstances would be burdened with extreme anxiety as he prepares for the final moment. Failure could be catastrophic, causing humiliation to his family and derision from his friends. The child's self-image could be shattered and irreparably damaged.

We Jews celebrate rather than test. We rejoice in watching as a little boy or girl grows up and matures, preparing to become an adult. Our "achievement" test, if anything, is one of mastery of knowledge and understanding of tradition. The call to the Torah is an honor, not a challenge to the child.

The fact of major significance is the realization that *Bar/Bat Mitzvah* is not really an event or an action. Thus it is not really a ritual. Rather, it is a condition or status. The words mean son/daughter of the commandments, i.e., one who is subject to the observance of the commandments. In a technical sense, one becomes *Bar* or *Bat Mitzvah* without even being in the synagogue and, believe it or not, without even having a large catered celebration. At the same time, the term *Bar* or *Bat Mitzvah* does not necessarily mean a young boy or girl. Since it is a condition, reflecting one's legal relationship to Jewish Law, an 80-year-old person is just as much a *Bar Mitzvah* as is a thirteen-year-old boy or a twelve-year-old girl. Because becoming a *Bar* or *Bat Mitzvah* is a condition rather than merely a ritual, some synagogues offer the opportunity for adults to become B'nai *Mitzvah*. For them, this is an opportunity to affirm or re-affirm their connection to Judaism. (However, for purposes of this discussion, we will refer to *Bar/Bat mitzvah* as a ritual—the actual ceremony.)

Bar Mitzvah seems to be a relatively recent phenomenon, dating from the Middle Ages. The child is called up to the Torah for an *aliyah* (nowadays, it is usually the last *aliyah* or *maftir aliyah*, leading into the *Haftarah*, the reading from the Prophets). This would be the child's first public demonstration of having reached his or her new status as a full member of the community. In some congregations, the parents may recite the following blessing:

> *"Praised are You, Adonai our God, who rules the universe, who has freed us of some responsibilities and conferred new ones upon _____"*

This statement can be understood in two ways:

1. Relief on the part of the parents that they are no longer responsible for the acts of their child.
2. Pride that their child is now an accepted adult within the community.

Since the ceremony revolves around an *aliyah* to the Torah, the *Bar/Bat Mitzvah* can take place any time that the Torah is read—Saturday *minha*, Monday and Thursday morning, *Rosh Chodesh* (the new month), as well as on *Shabbat* morning.

Many Conservative congregations have now adopted the Confirmation service. These services are usually held on the festival of *Shavuot*, since according to tradition, that day marks the giving of the Torah on Mount Sinai. Thus, there is a natural connection to the idea of transmitting Torah to the children. The disadvantage of this ceremony is that its format is one of a class commencement. We thus lose the idea of having a day set aside for each individual, in which he or she is the "star of the show," and is made to feel important and special.

The *Bat Mitzvah* is an even later development than the *Bar Mitzvah*. It was apparently introduced in France and Italy and soon spread to other countries. Rabbi Mordecai Kaplan, founder of the Reconstructionist Movement, was one of the proponents of equalizing the *Bat Mitzvah* with the *Bar Mitzvah*. Many synagogues have different customs for this ceremony. Many Conservative congregations hold them on Saturday morning with no difference from the *Bar Mitzvah*. Some have the girl recite a *Haftarah* on Friday evening. Others merely call her up for a special prayer, or allow her to lead the *Havdallah* service on Saturday evening.

Discussion

1. Is 12 or 13 an appropriate age to become an adult? Should the *Bar/Bat Mitzvah* ceremony be changed to age sixteen or some other age?

2. Imagine yourself to be celebrating your *Bar/Bat Mitzvah* again. You are expected to deliver a short talk during the service. Write down (or discuss) what you would say.

3. It is the night before your brother's *Bar Mitzvah* or sister's *Bat Mitzvah*. What kinds of things would you tell him/her?

4. If you had to live your *Bar/Bat Mitzvah* over again, would you do anything differently?

5. Traditionally, becoming a *Bar* or *Bat Mitzvah* means taking on the obligation to observe Jewish law. Do you think it still means the same thing in your community? If not, what does it symbolize?

6. How did you feel about Judaism at your *Bar/Bat Mitzvah* celebration? Did you feel like you were any different after the ceremonies than you were beforehand?

7. How is becoming a *Bar/Bat Mitzvah* different or similar to your transition to adulthood in the secular world? What are some of the symbols that represent becoming a Jewish adult and becoming an adult in North American society?

8. Are you in a confirmation program in your synagogue? What is the difference between a confirmation and a *Bar/Bat Mitzvah* celebration?

9. Do you know anyone who had an adult *Bar/Bat Mitzvah*? How was it different than a *Bar/Bat Mitzvah* for a 12 or 13 year old?

A MIRACLE *BAR MITZVAH*[8]

Nearly 1,000 people crowded into the sanctuary at Syracuse, New York's Temple Adath Yeshurun on June 10, 1994 for Eyal Sherman's *Bar Mitzvah*. What was remarkable about this *Bar Mitzvah* is that Eyal has been a quadriplegic and ventilator dependent since the age of four. He cannot breathe on his own, walk, talk or eat. And yet, this remarkable young man learned to read Hebrew, mouth the words of his *Haftarah*, and attended the community Hebrew high school. Eyal attended *Shabbat* services every Saturday morning and was an active member of his Kadima chapter.

Eyal's *Bar Mitzvah* was made technically possible by using video cameras to project his picture on a large screen. Congregants watched the screen which showed both the text and Eyal's face, thus were able to follow along while he moved his lips. In the same way that most kids use

---

[8] Excerpted from "A Miracle Kadimanik", Kol Kadima, Winter 1995, United Synagogue Youth

microphones as a way to amplify their voices in large synagogues, the video cameras "amplified" Eyal's means of communication—his facial expressions and lip movements. This system worked so well that people responded to Eyal just as they would have at any other *Bar* or *Bat Mitzvah*. The utter silence with which Eyal mouthed his prayers was followed by the thunderous responding chant from the congregation.

Eyal's achievements reflect the courage and devotion of his family, friends, teachers, doctors, and the many others who believe he should be given all the love, support and opportunities possible. Because of this support, Eyal excels in his studies at a regular public school, plays third base on a baseball team for the disabled, and has been recognized as a "*Mitzvah* Hero" by USY and Kadima's Danny Siegel. His father, Rabbi Charles Sherman of Temple Adath Yeshurun described the *Bar Mitzvah* as an opportunity for the community to look through a window "to see something special, not something freakish".

The word "special" only begins to describe Eyal, who like most Kadimaniks gave a speech during his *bar mitzvah*…

"Shabbat Shalom! Some people never thought I would have a Bar Mitzvah *because I'm in a wheelchair and on a respirator. But this day proves them wrong! You might think this is like a miracle, when something happens that you don't expect. Here I am today on the* bimah *(pulpit), an honor and a pleasure to be where my father stands each week. I prepared for my* Bar Mitzvah *at home for a long time starting when I was very young. I've learned to say the* Kiddush, *blessing over the wine, and* Birkat Hamazon, *grace after meals. My family builds a* Succah *every year and we put on our ski jackets and eat in it. I learned the prayers by coming to services every Shabbat with my family. It was harder for me to prepare than other kids. The Cantor had to learn to read my lips.*

Having my Bar Mitzvah *means I am now a man and now my father can call me on the phone to help make up the minyan when they are short. The happiest part of this day is having my relatives and friends from all over America and Israel here with me.*

Even though my Bar Mitzvah *is different, or awesome or radical, being high tech, I never really thought about that.*

I just always knew that when I reached age 13, I'd be up here on the bimah *and have a* Bar Mitzvah *just like any other kid."*

Eyal's story has received plenty of media coverage, from local newspapers, Jewish publications, and even CNN. And yet beyond all of this attention there is a much more basic lesson to be learned. Eyal tells all of us that the word impossible is just that—impossible. Anything is possible; anything is within hand's reach. At publication, Eyal is an upperclassman at Syracuse University as an Studio Art History major, minoring in Judaic Studies.

PROJECT: PREPARING FOR YOUR *BAR/BAT MITZVAH*[9]

Some suggestions to make your *Bar* or *Bat Mitzvah* more meaningful:

1. Donate a portion of your gift money to Tzedakah

2. Donate the leftover food to a local shelter or soup kitchen

---

[9] Excerpted from 11 Ways USYers Can Change The World in Big Ways by Danny Siegel, Published by the Tikun Olam Program of United Synagogue Youth

3. Donate 3% of the cost of the party to MAZON—Jewish Response to Hunger, the North American Jewish organization that funds many projects for hungry people in the US, Canada, Israel and other countries.

4. Donate the flowers to old age residencies, hospitals, etc.

5. Have the guests bring cans of food or overcoats or sweaters or toys to the party, to be distributed afterwards to needy people.

CAN A DEAF PERSON HAVE AN ALIYAH?

A Halachic Dilemma

> *A person who is deaf and mute is not of sound mind.*
> *Babylonian Talmud, Hagigah 2b*

Why do you think the rabbis perceived deaf-mutism as a mental impairment and not just a physical disability? Was it the deafness or the mutism that influenced this decision?

> *A deaf person, a retarded person, and a minor [prior to bar mitzvah] cannot perform a religious duty on behalf of a group. This is the general principle: one who is not himself under obligation to perform a religious duty cannot perform it on behalf of a congregation.(Rashi's Commentary on Babylonian Talmud, Hagigah 3b)*

A religious obligation can often be fulfilled by saying, "Amen." Can you think of examples?

If a religious obligation can only be fulfilled by someone who is also obligated, what is the problem here?

הקורא את שמע ולא השמיע לאזנו – יצא רבי יוסי אומר: לא יצא.

> *If one recites the Shema without hearing what he says, he has fulfilled his obligation. Rabbi Yose says he has not fulfilled it. (Babylonian Talmud, Brachot 15a)*

Based upon the text of the Shema, Jews are obligated to say the Shema twice a day. Why do you think Rabbi Yose holds that you need to hear the Shema in order to fulfill your obligation to say it?

> *One must hear with one's ears what one utters with one's mouth, but if one did not hear, he still fulfills the obligation, as long as his lips utter [the words].(Shulchan Aruch, Hilchot Kriyaat Shema 62:2)*

1. **What is the conclusion drawn by this text? Can a person with mutism fulfill the obligation? A person with deafness? A person who has deafness and mutism?**

2. How might you relate this opinion to the fact that now many individuals who are mute are able to communicate through various forms of sign language?

3. Could a deaf individual have an *aliyah* if he or she signed the brachot even if no one else in the room understood sign language because then no one would know when to say 'amen'? Would this prevent a deaf individual from becoming a *Bar/Bat Mitzvah*?

Look ahead to your next major milestones; graduation from high school and from college.

Which are you looking forward to more?

At what point do you expect others to begin treating you as an "adult"?

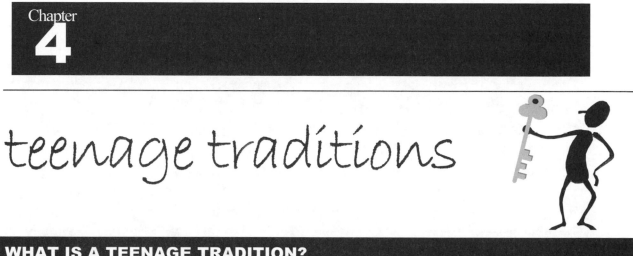

teenage traditions

WHAT IS A TEENAGE TRADITION?

As this volume was created, it became apparent that between *Bar* and *Bat Mitzvah* and Marriage, there was a void. When one is getting married, there are a many rituals to guide that process. Hopefully, a baby will soon follow, and there too, there are rituals. As that baby grows and becomes a *Bar* or *Bat Mitzvah*, again, Judaism has created a standard of practice—the *Bar* or *Bat Mitzvah* ceremony that takes place.

The teenage years bring with them a tremendous amount of growth, changes and new experiences. It seems fitting that there should be ceremonies and rituals that will evolve to incorporate Jewish *tradition* into our every day lives.

What events or stages might you think there should be a ritual or ceremony for during the teenage years?

COUNTED IN THE MINYAN AND THE MINI-VAN[10]

Although the *Bar* or *Bat Mitzvah* is the beginning of religious adulthood, our culture affords few meaningful opportunities for a 12 or 13-year-old to assert this new religious responsibility. Aside from being counted in a *minyan*, and perhaps being given the opportunity to lead worship or read Torah at one's synagogue, this new status does not often permeate one's daily life.

In our culture, many teens find that getting a driver's license is a much more meaningful rite of passage. With this license comes a real sense of responsibility, one that is expressed in a public way every time you get behind the wheel of a car. It is the first time that you literally have power of life and death over yourselves and others. A poor decision behind the wheel could result in injury or death for you, your friends or relatives, or even strangers. A decision to drink, or not to, is similarly serious.

In Congregation Temple Emunah, our rabbi, Rabbi Bernard Eisenman wrote a short ceremony. The new driver is called to the Torah, and the following prayer is recited.

---

[10] Contributed by David Srebnick

PRAYER UPON RECEIVING A DRIVER'S LICENSE

by Rabbi Bernard Eisenman, Temple Emunah, Lexington, Massachusetts

For a group:	*For a female:*	*For a male:*
אֱלֹהֵינוּ וֵאלֹהֵי אֲבוֹתֵינוּ	אֱלֹהֵינוּ וֵאלֹהֵי אֲבוֹתֵינוּ	אֱלֹהֵינוּ וֵאלֹהֵי אֲבוֹתֵינוּ
וְאִמּוֹתֵינוּ שְׁלַח בְּרָכָה	וְאִמּוֹתֵינוּ שְׁלַח בְּרָכָה	וְאִמּוֹתֵינוּ שְׁלַח בְּרָכָה
וְהַצְלָחָה לִבְנֵי וּבְנוֹת	וְהַצְלָחָה לְ_____ בַּת	וְהַצְלָחָה לְ_____ בֶּן
הַקְּהִילָה שֶׁקִּבְּלוּ רִשְׁיוֹן	_____ שֶׁקִּבְּלָה רִשְׁיוֹן	_____ שֶׁקִּבֵּל רִשְׁיוֹן
נְהִיגָת. הָגֵן יהוה עֲלֵיהֶם	נְהִיגָת. הָגֵן יהוה עָלֶיהָ	נְהִיגָת. הָגֵן יהוה עָלָיו וְתֵן
וְתֵן רוּחַ בִּינָה וְהַשְׂכֵּל	וְתֵן רוּחַ בִּינָה וְהַשְׂכֵּל	רוּחַ בִּינָה וְהַשְׂכֵּל לִנְהִיגָתוֹ
לִנְהִיגָתָם בַּדֶּרֶךְ. יִשְׁמֹר	לִנְהִיגָתָהּ בַּדֶּרֶךְ. יִשְׁמֹר	בַּדֶּרֶךְ. יִשְׁמוֹר יהוה אֶת
יהוה אֶת דַּרְכֵיהֶם שֶׁלֹּא	יהוה אֶת דְּרָכֶיהָ שֶׁלֹּא	דְּרָכָיו שֶׁלֹּא יָבוֹאוּ עָלָיו
יָבוֹאוּ עֲלֵיהֶם מִכְשׁוֹל וָנֶזֶק	יָבוֹאוּ עָלֶיהָ מִכְשׁוֹל וָנֶזֶק	מִכְשׁוֹל וָנֶזֶק וְלֹא יִקְרֶה לוֹ
וְלֹא יִקְרֶה לָהֶם אָסוֹן	וְלֹא יִקְרֶה לָהּ אָסוֹן בַּדֶּרֶךְ.	אָסוֹן בַּדֶּרֶךְ. וְיַגִּיעַ לִמְחוֹז
בַּדֶּרֶךְ. וְיַגִּיעוּ לִמְחוֹז חֶפְצָם	וְתַגִּיעַ לִמְחוֹז חֶפְצָה	חֶפְצוֹ בְּשָׁלוֹם וּבִשְׁלֵימוּת.
בְּשָׁלוֹם וּבִשְׁלֵימוּת. וְנֹאמַר	בְּשָׁלוֹם וּבִשְׁלֵימוּת. וְנֹאמַר	וְנֹאמַר אָמֵן.
אָמֵן.	אָמֵן.	

For all:

יְבָרֶכְךָ יהוה וְיִשְׁמְרֶךָ. יָאֵר יהוה פָּנָיו אֵלֶיךָ וִיחֻנֶּךָ.
יִשָּׂא יהוה פָּנָיו אֵלֶיךָ וְיָשֵׂם לְךָ שָׁלוֹם.

Almighty God, we seek Your blessings on _____ who has/have received a driver's license. May You bless him/her/them with understanding, discretion, and knowledge. May he/she/they always be polite and cautious on the roads he/she/they travel(s). May the parents of this/these newly licensed driver(s) know a sense of security and peace during these times. We pray that _____ appreciate(s) the privilege of driving by following all laws pertaining to operating a motor vehicle. May he/she/they reach all destinations in wholeness of body and mind. May all his/her/their driving experiences be moments of safety, sobriety, joy, and happiness. Amen.

May the Lord bless you and keep you.

May the Lord cause His countenance to shine upon you and be gracious to you.

May the Lord turn his countenance to you and grant you peace.

Driver says:
You are my shelter, You will preserve me from trouble,
You will surround me with songs of deliverance. Selah.
　　　(Psalms 32:7)

Driver says:

אַתָּה סֵתֶר לִי מִצַּר תִּצְּרֵנִי
רָנֵּי פַלֵּט תְּסוֹבְבֵנִי סֶלָה.
Atah seiter li mitzar titzreini
ranei faleit t'sov'veini selah.

How does this ceremony make the driver's license …

A Cause For Rejoicing	Something that tied me to tradition	Something that made me feel important	Something that helps Jewish unity

CHOOSING A COLLEGE JEWISHLY

By Richard Moline

A first year college student, worried about where he will go for the high holidays, phones home from his mid-western university just prior to Rosh Hashanah. The few Jewish students on campus are not particularly organized and he does not know whom to call to see if there is a synagogue nearby. At a small liberal arts college, a student tells her parents that she has a midterm during Pesach and will not be able to go home for the *s'darim* because her professor will not let her delay the test. Another student at a large state school talks about anti-Semitic speakers who are often paid from the student activities fund (i.e., tuition dollars).

Panicked, concerned parents all too often find out that little, if anything, can be done to help their child. "'If only we had known," they proclaim, "we would have pointed them towards a different school." Frustrated, students may spend a miserable semester or year, or even find themselves transferring to another school where they might feel more comfortable being Jewish.

The college selection process, while opening doors to unparalleled growth and exploration, can also be very stressful and trying. Scores of books are published each year providing students and their parents with information on various schools, their academic requirements, financial aid, and other concerns. Most families explore these areas quite carefully while neglecting to consider the availability of any Jewish programming or community.

Even for the most firmly committed, maintaining a strong Jewish connection on today's college campus is difficult. The familiarity and comfort of home is replaced with uncertainty. Students suddenly need to make countless decisions resulting from their new-found independence: study habits must be fashioned; courses need to be selected; there are new friends to make; money to be managed; social, academic and extracurricular opportunities to explore; and intellectual challenges to be met.

The strain of anti-Jewish activity on some campuses adds to the ambivalence many students feel about their own Judaism. In addition to anti-Semitic speakers, articles appear in student newspapers questioning the legitimacy of the Holocaust. Israel Independence Day celebrations are disrupted by fellow students questioning Israel's right to exist. Members of other faiths challenge fundamental Jewish beliefs. With all of these pressures, the Jewish component of student life is often put on hold.

Parents and students should begin talking about college-related issues before the junior year in high school. When looking for a college or university, location, academics, population, size, and finances are naturally considered, knowing that different students have different needs. Family circumstances, academic achievements and college test scores also affect the options. And while everything might look good on paper, both students and their parents must be aware that the reality of university life may be completely different.

There are certain questions each Jewish family must ask when looking at schools. It is important to know in advance the population and percentage of Jewish students on campus. While students should not limit themselves to only Jewish friends and acquaintances, it is comforting to know that there will be others with similar backgrounds who share common experiences. It is just as essential to know which institutions on campus are available to support the Jewish population.

- Is there an active Hillel Foundation (or its equivalent)?

- Who are the professional staff?

- What *Shabbat* and holiday activities, student groups, kosher meal plans, etc. are offered?

- Is there a KOACH group for Conservative Jewish students? Is there a Jewish community nearby?

- Are there job possibilities in a local synagogue as a religious school teacher or USY advisor?

- Are Jewish studies courses offered?

- Will you be able to receive credit for a year of study in Israel?

- How does the university respect Jewish observance in relation to the school's calendar?

- Many fraternities and sororities are no longer exclusively Jewish. If this type of living arrangement is best for you, is it available?

Moreover, parents and children need to discuss Jewish issues prior to attending college (whether living at home or on campus). What are the expectations in terms of inter-dating? Where should a student go if confronted by a missionary? For which holidays is the student expected to be home?

A careful examination of these issues may help avoid some (but not all) potential problems for Jewish students. While there are many challenges, there are also numerous colleges and universities which provide a vibrant Jewish life, including an actively involved Jewish faculty.

A family should conduct a proper investigation of any college it is considering on a variety of levels. The admissions office of many colleges and universities will have population statistics. The campus Hillel Foundation or Jewish Student Union is another good source of information. Speak with the director, and obtain the names of actively involved students who are generally happy to talk with potential recruits. Often, a fellow student can answer certain questions far better than an admissions officer or Hillel director.

As a final step in the decision-making process, visit the campus. Arrive towards the end of the week in order to observe classes and ensure appointments with university personnel. Make arrangements to stay on the campus for *Shabbat*. This often serves as a *bar*ometer of Jewish life.

Students should feel secure in knowing that their Judaism need not be compromised at the college of their choice. With prior investigation and dialogue, students should be able to graduate, not only with a diploma, but with their Jewish identity intact.

LECH LECHA—A Ceremony of Going Forth[11]

College is a time of unparalleled exploration and discovery. Campus life presents a whirlwind of changes. The following prayers are offered as students receive aliyot to the Torah before going off to college.

May God Who blessed our ancestors, Abraham, Isaac and Jacob, Sarah, Rebecca, Rachel and Leah, bless _____ as they embark on this significant and transforming journey. Give them strength to meet the challenges which lie ahead and the wisdom to choose well at every junction. May their heritage and tradition be the signposts which guide them on their way. Give them the courage to ask questions, seek knowledge and better our world. "Lekh lekha me-artzecha—Go forth from your land," God told Abraham, "Go forth from your native land, from your father's house, to the land which I will show you... va-avarkheka... and I will bless you." May, _____, too, always feel God's sheltering presence.

Parents recite the following:

We have given you roots and wings. Take them, with our love, and use them well.

May God bless you and keep you	יְבָרֶכְךָ יְיָ וְיִשְׁמְרֶךָ:
May God be with you and be gracious unto you.	יָאֵר יְיָ פָּנָיו אֵלֶיךָ וִיחֻנֶּךָּ:
May God show you kindness and give you peace.	יִשָּׂא יְיָ פָּנָיו אֵלֶיךָ וְיָשֵׂם לְךָ שָׁלוֹם:

Students recite *T'filat HaDerekh:*

יְהִי רָצוֹן מִלְפָנֶיךָ יְיָ אֱלֹהֵינוּ וֵאלֹהֵי אֲבוֹתֵינוּ, שֶׁתּוֹלִיכֵנוּ לְשָׁלוֹם
וְתַצְעִידֵנוּ לְשָׁלוֹם וְתַדְרִיכֵנוּ לְשָׁלוֹם וְתַגִּיעֵנוּ לִמְחוֹז חֶפְצֵנוּ לְחַיִּים
וּלְשִׂמְחָה וּלְשָׁלוֹם וְתַחֲזִירֵנוּ לְבֵיתֵנוּ לְשָׁלוֹם וְתַצִּילֵנוּ
מִכַּף כָּל אוֹיֵב וְאוֹרֵב בַּדֶּרֶךְ וּמִכָּל מִינֵי
פֻּרְעָנִיּוֹת הַמִּתְרַגְּשׁוֹת לָבוֹא לָעוֹלָם, וְתִשְׁלַח בְּרָכָה (בְּכָל) מַעֲשֵׂה
יָדֵינוּ, וְתִתְּנֵנוּ לְחֵן וּלְחֶסֶד וּלְרַחֲמִים בְּעֵינֶיךָ וּבְעֵינֵי כָל רוֹאֵינוּ,
וְתִשְׁמַע קוֹל תַּחֲנוּנֵינוּ, כִּי אֵל שׁוֹמֵעַ תְּפִלָּה וְתַחֲנוּן אָתָּה. בָּרוּךְ
אַתָּה יְיָ, שׁוֹמֵעַ תְּפִלָּה.

May it be Your will, Adonai our God and God of our ancestors, to guide us in peace, to sustain us in peace, to lead us to our desired destination in health and joy and peace, and to bring us home in peace. Save us from every enemy and disaster on the way, and from all calamities that threaten the

---

[11] Created by Koach, a project of the United Synagogue of Conservative Judaism. Used with permission.

world. Bless the work of our hands. May we find grace, love and compassion in Your sight and in the sight of all who see us. Hear our supplication, for You listen to prayer and supplication. Praised are You, Adonai, Who hears prayer. Amen.

How does this ceremony make going off to college …

A Cause For Rejoicing	Something that tied me to tradition	Something that made me feel important	Something that helps Jewish unity

CREATING NEW RITUALS

The ceremony for getting a driver's license or for going off to college are unique responses to modern-day life cycle events. The authors of both ceremonies recognized that there are many more life cycle events aside from the traditional ones.

If you had to create a ceremony for a life cycle event, could you? What might you put into it?

Look at the following list of events and see if you can draft a ceremony that could be used with it. Feel free to incorporate any of the elements of the ceremonies that we have already introduced in this book.

Going to Israel	Returning from Israel
Getting into college	Graduating Jr. High School or High School
Receiving a prestigious award	Getting bad news about one's health
Recovering from illness	Finishing chemotherapy
Going to camp	Coming home from camp
First time away from home	Doing something scary
Asking for courage to do something important	Moving into a new home (m'zuzah blessing)
Deciding to get serious with a boy/girl friend	Beginning to menstruate
Having a baby	Adopting a child (i.e., getting a new sibling)

Wearing new clothing

Getting a new job

Leaving a job

Getting a good grade; improving one's average

Becoming disabled

Getting your first job

Losing a job

Being elected to a USY office

Getting good news: making a team, getting a role in a play

Suicide (attempted or successful)

_____

_____

_____

_____

_____

_____

_____

_____

_____

_____

_____

_____

_____

_____

finding a mate

A [Roman] matron asked R. Jose: "In how many days did the Holy One, blessed be He, create His world?" "In six days," he answered. "Then what has He been doing since then?" "He sits and makes matches," he answered, "assigning this man to that woman, and this woman to that man." "If that is difficult," she gibed, "I too can do the same." She went and matched [her slaves], giving this man to that woman, this woman to that man and so on. Some time after those who were thus united went and beat one another, this woman saying, "I do not want this man: while this man protested, "I do not want that woman."' Straightway she summoned R. Jose b. Halafta and admitted to him: "There is no god like your God: it is true, your Torah is indeed beautiful and praiseworthy, and you spoke the truth!" (Bereishit Rabbah 68:4)

As the Roman noblewoman in the story discovered, finding your *bashert* (literally, predestined, this usually refers to your soul mate or the person God intends you to marry) is not as simple as some movies may have us believe. Whether or not you believe in love at first sight, a lot goes into choosing a spouse.

Naturally, Judaism has a lot to say about the subject of choosing a spouse. In the source below, we are encouraged to find a spouse who is of a similar age.

If he, for instance, was young and she old, or if he was old and she was young, he is told, "What would you with a young woman?" or "What would you with an old woman?" "Go to one who is [of the same age] as yourself and create no strife in your house!"

(Babylonian Talmud, Tractate Yevamot 44a)

This suggests that greater compatibility is found between those who are at similar stages of life. While popular culture has often stated that opposites attract, many relationships are formed because people share similar backgrounds and therefore similar values and experiences.

LOOKING BACK

1. **In the past, you may have been interested in establishing a close relationship with another teenager. When you have been interested in someone, what has that interest been based on? Looks? Personality? Intelligence?**

2. **What first attracted you to these other people?**

 **Look at your answer above.**

Now, think about the qualities you want in the person who you might eventually marry. Are the qualities the same as those that attracted you to other people? Why or why not?

Judaism also had its own version of the "Dating Game" where single men and women could meet each other.

אָמַר רַבָּן שִׁמְעוֹן בֶּן גַּמְלִיאֵל, לֹא הָיוּ יָמִים טוֹבִים לְיִשְׂרָאֵל כַּחֲמִשָּׁה עָשָׂר בְּאָב וּכְיוֹם הַכִּפּוּרִים, שֶׁבָּהֶן בְּנוֹת יְרוּשָׁלַיִם יוֹצְאוֹת בִּכְלֵי לָבָן שְׁאוּלִין, שֶׁלֹּא לְבַיֵּשׁ אֶת מִי שֶׁאֵין לוֹ. כָּל הַכֵּלִים טְעוּנִין טְבִילָה. וּבְנוֹת יְרוּשָׁלַיִם יוֹצְאוֹת וְחוֹלוֹת בַּכְּרָמִים. וּמֶה הָיוּ אוֹמְרוֹת, בָּחוּר, שָׂא נָא עֵינֶיךָ וּרְאֵה, מָה אַתָּה בּוֹרֵר לָךְ. אַל תִּתֵּן עֵינֶיךָ בַּנּוֹי, תֵּן עֵינֶיךָ בַּמִּשְׁפָּחָה. (משלי לא)

Rabban Shimon ben Gamliel said, There were no holidays for Israel as the fifteenth of Av (Tu b'Av) and as Yom Kippur, for on them the daughters of Jerusalem go forth in borrowed white garments, so as not to embarrass whoever does not have...And the daughters of Jerusalem go forth and dance in the vineyards. And what would they say? "Young man, lift up your eyes and see, what you choose for yourself. Do not set your eyes on beauty, set your eyes on the family: 'Grace is deceitful, and beauty is vain, but a woman that fears the Lord, she shall be praised' (Prov. 31:30).(Mishnah, Tractate Ta'anit 4:8)

Do you think that wealth, beauty and status should even be considered when choosing a spouse, or should they be off limits? Why?

It is interesting to note that rather than promoting the cultural deal of "keeping up with the Joneses" this text emphasizes attributes other than wealth and physical beauty. The suitors are encouraged to consider how the woman was raised and the values that she holds.

1. **In what ways could spouses from different family backgrounds have issues that come up specifically because of those differences?**

2. **You have gone through your own list of qualities that you would look for in a potential mate. How does your list compare with those that these texts seem to be concentrating on?**

3. **Do you agree with the Jewish ideas of who is a good person to marry and who is not?**

4. **The text above seems to be describing a singles event from about 2,000 years ago. What are the advantages and disadvantages of choosing a spouse quickly, but without knowing background information such as financial or family status?**

In today's world, pressure to date, if not dating itself, begins in the teenage years. High school students often forge meaningful and significant relationships with others their age that become an integral part of their respective lives. Each Jewish teenager should begin to give serious thought to creating a dating ethic. Two considerations demonstrate the need to create such an ethic, that is, a set of rules for making good decisions.

First, one should be consciously aware that while only a minority of people end up marrying their high school sweetheart, some people in fact do end up doing exactly that! As such, for any teenager to assume that one's relationship with one's partner is short term, might in fact simply be a mistake. There are those who date the same person from high school through college and beyond, even though perhaps separated by significant distances during the courtship. Not every teenage romance is short-lived. It is not unheard of that a couple might form the foundation of a lasting and serious relationship while in high school.

For the majority of people however, teenage relationships do not lead directly to marriage. As such, it might fairly be asked what impact, if any, a teenager's dating ethic has upon family structure. While several possibilities might soundly respond to this question, one answer seems to clearly evolve from classical Rabbinic thought.

בֶּן עַזַּאי אוֹמֵר, הֱוֵי רָץ לְמִצְוָה קַלָּה (כְּבַחֲמוּרָה), וּבוֹרֵחַ מִן הָעֲבֵרָה. שֶׁמִּצְוָה גּוֹרֶרֶת מִצְוָה, וַעֲבֵרָה גוֹרֶרֶת עֲבֵרָה. שֶׁשְּׂכַר מִצְוָה, מִצְוָה. וּשְׂכַר עֲבֵרָה, עֲבֵרָה:

One should run to fulfill a minor commandment as if it were a major one and flee from any transgression; for one mitzvah leads to another mitzvah, while one sin leads to yet another sin. The reward for doing a mitzvah is another mitzvah while the reward for one sin is yet another sin. (Pirke Avot 4:2)

According to this mishnah, humans are creatures of habit. Psychological studies have repeatedly shown that past behavior is the best predictor of future performance. Just as New Year's resolutions are quickly forgotten, we tend to repeat the behaviors that we have already done. The type of person who you say is okay to date today is more than likely to have an impact on the type of person who you think is okay to date in the future when more serious relationships develop. As such, even one's earliest dating patterns play a significant role in influencing one's future and the future of one's family.

As with any other important pursuit, the preparation affects the final result. If working hard at practices results in a better played game, if doing homework results in a particular type of grade, if being a good person makes the world a better place, then certainly, who and how you date today can affect who you marry tomorrow.

In any dating situation decisions must be made which impact profoundly upon one's life. Who one decides to date and the type of relationship which one decides to pursue will have consequences. It would be wise for anyone dating or considering dating to thoughtfully assess where the results of their decisions might lead. The important thing about dating is that we learn how to build and sustain intimate relationships. We learn to give of ourselves, to compromise, to listen, to empathize, to love, and to be honest. We learn to express difficult emotions, to take risks, etc.

Through dating, we discover what is important to us in a relationship, and what is important to others.

While there is room for latitude in dating, certain standards are fundamental in Judaism. Rabbi Elliot Dorff addressed many of these issues in "This is My Beloved, This is My Friend: A Rabbinic Letter on Intimate Relations." Three messages are clear about dating within Judaism:

A. Jewish law forbids intermarriage without exception. This bears upon a Jew's dating ethic; dating only Jews enhances the potential of a Jewish marriage and raising Jewish children. While no legal code explicitly forbids dating non-Jews, this is because such activity is not entertained in Jewish law as a legitimate option.

B. As the most intimate and holy of acts, intercourse is reserved for the most intimate and holy relationships. Ultimate intimacy is tied to ultimate commitment and therefore, marriage is the appropriate context for sexual intercourse. From a Jewish perspective full commitment and the development of the emotional and spiritual relationship must precede physical intimacy.

C. Every person, male or female, must not be objectified, but rather treated as a valued soul, created in the image of God. To treat a partner, a date, or indeed anyone without expressing the highest concern for their integrity and inherent holiness is nothing less then a sin.

A SPECIAL NOTE CONCERNING TEENAGERS[12]

If the above considerations apply to adults, they apply all the more to teenagers, for whom the commitments of marriage and children are simply not possible. This, though, puts such people in an especially difficult bind, for the level of sexual hormones in their bodies is as high as it will ever get. We rabbis recognize that teenagers throughout history have been driven by their hormones to seek each other's company and to explore their sexuality. The Conservative Movement has therefore created, and will continue to create, opportunities for Jewish teenagers to meet each other and to learn to feel comfortable in each other's presence. As long as the relationship is voluntary on the part of both partners, and as long as Judaism's norms of modesty and privacy are maintained, holding hands, hugging, and kissing are as legitimate for teenagers as they build romantic relationships they are for older people.

Even more than single adults, though, teenagers need to refrain from sexual intercourse, for they cannot honestly deal with its implications or results-- including the commitments and responsibilities that sexual relations normally imply, the possibility of children, and the risk of AIDS and other sexually transmitted diseases. Abstinence is surely not easy when the physical and social pressures are strong, but it is the only responsible thing to do.

One other matter.... we want to reaffirm here our belief that Jewish teenagers should date Jews exclusively. As much as marriage may seem eons away, dating is the usual way in which young people meet and ultimately marry. Marrying the boy or girl next door is still a common phenomenon, for such people share experiences from their high school years and perhaps even from early childhood, and so high school students need to restrict their dates to Jews.

---

[12] Excerpted with Permission from the Rabbinical Assembly. Rabbi Elliot Dorff, p 36, "This is My Beloved, This Is My Friend:" A Rabbinic Letter on Intimate Relations. A paper of the Commission on Human Sexuality. The Rabbinical Assembly, 1996.

Along the same lines, high school juniors and seniors planning for college should be sure to choose a school with a significant number of Jews. That is important for general religious, educational, and social reasons, but the romantic factor is absolutely critical. Many people do not find their mate in college, but a significant number do, and so one important element in a Jew's choice of college should be the availability of other Jews with whom one can form a community and among whom one can date.

For Discussion

1. **Judaism clearly places a priority on finding a spouse, but not everyone chooses to marry. Why do you think that some people stay single? What would Jewish tradition say about people who stayed single?**

2. **Is it better to stay single or to marry a non-Jew?**

3. **How should the Jewish community reach out to single Jews?**

4. **There are several Internet-based dating services designed for Jews to meet other Jews. How do you feel about this method of meeting?**

5. **Some Jewish groups organize "shiduchim" or matches for single Jews. How do you feel about this?**

6. **Let's say that you meet your soul mate and have decided to get married. As part of getting a civil wedding license (required by law), some states require the couple to have a blood test to look for sexually transmitted diseases. Some couples choose to have a genetic screening done to see if either is a carrier for a specific disease, e.g. Tay Sachs. What do you do if you discover that a potential partner is a carrier for a genetically transmitted disorder?[13]**

7. **If your friend says he's opposed to intermarriage but decided to inter-date anyway, at what point in the relationship should he disclose the fact that he would not intermarry?**

8. **There are those who say that they would never intermarry, but think that inter-dating is OK because there is no intent at the time of the date to get married. Although dating does not always lead to marriage, there is an expectation that it could lead to a serious relationship and to some long-term commitment to an exclusive relationship (perhaps months or even years). If a friend decided to inter-date, would you counsel her to disclose her preference about intermarriage at the beginning of the relationship? Should she say to her date: "I'd like to go out with you and get to know you, but we can't get serious because I will only marry someone who is Jewish."?**

In any dating situation decisions must be made which impact profoundly upon one's life. Who one decides to date and the type of relationship which one decides to pursue will have consequences. It would be wise for anyone dating or considering dating to thoughtfully asses

---

[13] Tay Sachs Disease—This is a rare genetic disorder that causes fatty substances to build up on neurons. Subsequently, physical and mental developments are stunted. This is followed by convulsions, blindness, and death. There is no cure for Tay Sachs. To have the disease, the child must inherit a gene for the disease from both parents. A person who has received the gene from only one parent is referred to as a carrier. Tay Sachs carriers are most commonly found among Ashkenazi Jews (Central and Eastern European descent). It is possible to screen for the gene through a blood sample.

where the results of their decisions might lead. In *Pirke Avot*, Rabbi Yochanan asks of his disciples (2:13):

אָמַר לָהֶם, צְאוּ וּרְאוּ אֵיזוֹהִי דֶרֶךְ יְשָׁרָה שֶׁיִּדְבַּק בָּהּ הָאָדָם.

Go out and discover what is the good path which one should adhere to in life.

When his students return, Rabbi Shimon wisely states,

רַבִּי שִׁמְעוֹן אוֹמֵר, הָרוֹאֶה אֶת הַנּוֹלָד.

One should envision the consequences of one's actions.

Everyone is seeking something different in their soul mate.

Below is a list of "qualities" that can exist in a future husband or wife. How many of them are important to you? Could you pick your top five?

☐ Beautiful/Handsome	☐ Jewish Education	☐ Mentally Stable
☐ Sense of Humor	☐ Romantic	☐ Intelligent Taste in Clothing
☐ Common Interests/Activities	☐ Has Money	☐ Taste in Music
☐ Outgoing	☐ Wants Kids	☐ Kind
☐ Observant of *Shabbat*	☐ Good Relationship with His/Her Family	☐ Jewish
☐ Observant of Kashrut	☐ Good to Talk to	☐ Good Dancer
☐ Artistic	☐ Fun	☐ Understanding

Each of us has set limits about who we will and will not date.

WOULD YOU DATE SOMEONE WHO?	WHAT ARE THE CONSEQUENCES?
Lives in another city?	
Insists on seeing you at least 3 times every week?	
Your parents do not approve of, for whatever reason?	
Your friends do not approve of, for whatever reason?	
Is in college now?	
Whose code of morality (right and wrong) is different from your own?	
Is less observant than you?	
Is more observant than you?	

Won't eat in your parent's house because it is not kosher?	
Goes to synagogue on a daily basis?	
Whose religion is different from your religion?	
Never goes or has no interest in going to synagogue?	
Refuses to give money to beggars on the street?	
Refuses to fast on Yom Kippur?	
Sees serious sexual activity as a necessary part of your relationship?	
Feels that physical intimacy should be left to the confines of marriage?	
Does not respect you as a Jew?	

the jewish wedding

Marriage, the unity of two souls into one, is unquestionably considered to be the ideal human state within the Jewish tradition. The Bible expresses this thought in the very beginning, when it states (referring to Adam and Eve);

עַל־כֵּן יַעֲזָב־אִישׁ אֶת־אָבִיו וְאֶת־אִמּוֹ וְדָבַק בְּאִשְׁתּוֹ וְהָיוּ לְבָשָׂר אֶחָד:

Hence a man leaves his father and mother and clings to his wife, so that they become one flesh.
(Bereishit 2:24)

The Christian Bible, on the other hand, considers celibacy as a higher ideal than marriage, which is a factor driving Christianity's attitude toward the sexual impulse. To some Christians, marriage is thought of as a concession to human weakness; the Rabbis, however, saw celibacy as unnatural. The Talmud says: "He who has no wife is not a proper man." In contrast to the Christian outlook on sex, the Talmud states: "Were it not for the sexual impulse, no man would build a house, marry a wife, or beget children." Thus, not only is marriage acceptable, but it is healthy and necessary for the proper development of human character and maturity.

1. **What do you think "become one flesh" means? Is this a reference to just the physical aspects of marriage?**

2. **In our day and age, do you feel that children have already left their parents before marriage?**

3. **In what ways can a marriage symbolize a more permanent change in the relationship between a person and his or her parents?**

4. **Why do you think Judaism puts such a strong emphasis on marriage?**

We can see the importance attached to marriage by our tradition by the use of certain metaphors and imagery. The prophets often referred to the relationship between God and Israel as that between husband and wife. An entire book of the Bible, Shir HaShirim (Song of Songs), utilizes explicit sexual imagery, which was later interpreted as a metaphor for the God-Israel relationship. The *Shabbat* is referred to as a bride in the Friday Evening liturgy.

We sing, "*Lecha dodi likrat kallah-* לְכָה דוֹדִי לִקְרַאת כַּלָּה --Come, my beloved, to greet the Sabbath bride."

1. **What about a Jew's relationship with *Shabbat* would we be trying to duplicate in a marriage?**

2. **What sort of parallels can you draw between *Shabbat* and marriage?**

Some religions or philosophies emphasize body over soul or soul over body. Judaism tries to strike a healthy balance, seeing the physical and spiritual as equally valid and important. We can see this difference demonstrated by the vocabulary of various civilizations. The Greeks had two words for the two possible manifestations of love:

agape—represents the spiritual type of love.

eros—represents the physical type of love.

Hebrew has only one word, *ahava*. In other words, we use the same word to describe our relationship with God as we do for describing sexual attraction. This concretizes the idea that we have always felt an interdependence of the physical and the spiritual, or what some call the profane and the holy. We believe that the physical world is capable of being raised to a spiritual level, that indeed spirituality is impossible without the tangible, material world. Thus, it should be no surprise that the Hebrew word for marriage is *kiddushin*, which contains within it the word *kadosh*—holy or sacred.

LOOKING BACK

1. **How did your parents meet?**

2. **What do you know about their wedding day? Do they ever talk about it?**

3. **Have you ever seen a picture of your parents wedding? What do you think of the clothing? What emotions does that picture convey to you?**

ENGAGEMENT/ TENAIM

The classical North American engagement typically involves the man dropping to one knee before his girlfriend in a romantic location. He presents her with a diamond ring and asks, "[Insert name of girlfriend here], will you marry me?" There is no direct Jewish equivalent for this particular event because Judaism views marriage as an event that involves family and community.

Historically, prior to the wedding, the families of the bride and groom would meet to agree to the conditions of the marriage. This was called the *Tena'im* (conditions). The families would sign a document stating the date and place of the proposed marriage and the financial obligations of the parties. This event was called *Erusin* or *Kiddushin* (betrothal or sanctification). Today, *Erusin*, the "engagement," is part of the wedding service, Tena'im is observed much less frequently. Those who do observe it often turn it into the equivalent of an engagement party or as part of the events surrounding the wedding date.

Reinventing Tradition—The Tenaim Ceremony[14]

It took God six days to create the world. A fair question, then, is: What has God been doing since that time? A midrash *(Bereshit Rabah 68:4) relates that precisely this question was asked of Rabbi Yose bar Halafta by a Roman woman. Rabbi Yose answered that since Creation, God is* m'zaveg zvugim -- *putting couples together. God is acting as a* shadkhan, *arranging marriages.*

The woman protested to Rabbi Yose that matchmaking was an easy task, hardly sufficient to take up God's time. To prove her point, she lined up a thousand males and a thousand females and arranged one thousand marriages.

The result? After one night they returned -- with a broken leg, a gouged eye, and a cracked head, among other injuries. Rabbi Yose advised the woman -- and countless future generations of anxious parents and potential shadkhanim -- *that even for God, the art of matchmaking was a miracle as incredible as the splitting of the Reed Sea.*

It is with such a realization that parents are understandably overjoyed when their children announce that they have met their bashert -- *their intended -- and are engaged and planning to wed. Whether through a simple* l'chayim *or a more elaborate engagement party, the couple and their parents are anxious to share their* simhah *with family and friends. It was in just such a position my wife and I found ourselves in the Spring of 2000 when our son Zev called from Israel with the announcement that he had asked Sharon to marry him -- and that she had said yes.*

Since the mid-winter wedding would be about eight months off, an early summer engagement party was planned. While the symbols and rituals of a Jewish wedding are well defined, not so the engagement party. There was, however, one suggestion I made which was promptly accepted by the couple – let us have a formal Tenaim.

Tenaim *is a Hebrew term meaning conditions or stipulations. In the context of an upcoming wedding, the term refers to a document, formalizing an agreement between the families. At one time, such documents recorded the* tenaim, *or conditions, governing the financial terms of the upcoming marriage. Such documents, entered into well before the wedding, formalized not only the engagement but everything else –from the cost of the wedding to what the bride and groom would bring into the marriage.*

While today there are couples who negotiate and even have lawyers prepare intricate civil pre-nuptial agreements, over time the detailed pre-marital Tenaim *fell into disuse. Ultimately, a more-or-less standardized form of the document developed. Even in traditional circles, however, this document is often ignored, and, when used, is signed as a merely symbolic act on the day of the wedding immediately before signing the ketubah.*

Why, then, did I suggest a formal Tenaim *to my son and future daughter-in-law some six or more months before the wedding? Perhaps Rabbi Avraham Isaac Kook (first Ashkenazi Chief Rabbi of modern Israel) said it best: "Ha'yashan yithadesh, he'hadash yitkadesh –That which is old should be made new, that which is new should be made holy." Our son's engagement gave us the opportunity to renew an old custom, the* Tenaim, *and to sanctify a new custom, the modern engagement party.*

The standard form of the Tenaim *document, addressed primarily to representatives of the groom and bride (traditionally, the fathers) confirms that the couple "has no claims or demands on the other" and that "they will be wed under the* huppah *and* kiddushin *(formal sanctification of the marriage) in accordance with the law of Moses and Israel" on a specified date. Knowing that sometimes plans change, we added a little flexibility to the date with the words "more or less as the parties may agree."*

---

[14] By Kenneth Goldrich, Excerpts reprinted with permission from The Review, United Synagogue of Conservative Judaism, Spring 2001

The couple further committed not to "not run away from each other or hide any facts about their finances, sharing authority equally in peace and tranquility."

We added two provisions to the standard text. First, "To further secure and strengthen" the Tenaim *"the* hatan *and kallah have themselves affixed their signatures." Second, we attempted to avoid a potential* halakhic *pitfall through another condition. A marriage is terminated by a* get. *A* Tenaim *is -- while not yet a marriage -- still a solemn contractual undertaking.*

An interesting provision in the Tenaim *relates to the* kenas, *or "fine," that must be paid if the agreement is broken. Although in our day and age the fine is purely symbolic, it underscores Judaism's insistence on the importance of words. To have the opportunity at an engagement party for the couple to publicly declare in front of friends and family their intentions of marriage gives expression to the sacredness of words and what words represent.*

The Tenaim *ceremony itself, while legal in nature, seems to transcend the technicalities of Jewish law and allows all those present to experience something very spiritual and transcendent. Before the plate was broken and the* Tenaim *concluded with singing and dancing, I asked those present to offer the engaged couple a* berakhah, *a word of blessing, a word of encouragement. Parents, relatives, and friends offered stirring and moving words which brought many of us to tears. Memories of those who had passed away and could not be there were invoked. It seemed as though the past, the present and the future merged at that moment when the hopes for this couple and their intention to fulfill their vows to marry each other were concretized. The breaking of the plate symbolically sealed before God and all those assembled the depth of their love and their commitment to each other, to Torah and to the Jewish people.*

Engagements do sometimes end prior to marriage. Thus, we included a liquidated damage provision providing for a fixed monetary payment (in our case, $50) by the party, God forbid, who called off the wedding.

The incorporation of a formal Tenaim *ceremony at the engagement party -- with a rabbi officiating -- made the fact of the engagement more solemn and added a level of* keshushah *to what might otherwise have been a purely secular party. During the ceremony, the fathers made a* kinyan *(formal acknowledgment by the symbolic holding of a handkerchief). The document was signed by two witnesses, and the rabbi gave a short charge to the couple and then read and translated the document. The final component of the* Tenaim *ceremony was the breaking of a plate, traditionally by the mothers. Just as shattered pottery cannot be reconstructed, neither can the difficulties of a broken engagement ever be fully repaired. Just as the shattering is final, so too should the engagement be final and lasting. Carefully wrapped in a pillow case (so the shards would not be scattered), the plate was smashed, followed by shouts of* mazel tov.

Unlike a wedding, there is much less structure to a Tenaim/*engagement ceremony. Thus, it lends itself to somewhat more creativity. Several of the groom's friends spoke, including one who had come in from Israel for the occasion and was given the honor of being an* eyd, *or witness, to the signing of the* Tenaim *document. I also spoke, tying in the week's Torah* parashah *(which, as luck would have it, was my bar mitzvah portion), with my hopes and prayers for the couple and their continuing commitment both to each other and to the people of Israel, the land of Israel and the God of Israel.*

Family, friends and food always enhance a simhah. *The* Tenaim *ceremony focused our thoughts and added a dimension that might otherwise have been overlooked on this joyous occasion.*

Questions to think about…

1. **In what way is this ritual meaningful?**

2. **What would you change or add to this ritual to make it more meaningful?**

3. Has your family ever used such a ritual? If so, what was different?

How is *Tenaim*...

A Cause For Rejoicing	Something that tied me to tradition	Something that made me feel important	Something that helps Jewish unity

BEFORE THE MARRIAGE

AUFRUF

A number of events and rituals take place in the days before the wedding ceremony. On the *Shabbat* before the wedding, there is an Aufruf (Yiddish for calling up), during which the groom is called to the Torah for an *aliyah*. In some synagogues, the couple is called up together for the *aliyah,* or the bride may be called up on her own. The rabbi of the synagogue may ask the couple how they met and recite a *Mi sheberach* blessing for the couple. It is the custom for the congregation to throw raisins and candies at the groom as he finishes his *aliyah*, with the hopes of ensuring a sweet life for the couple.

MIKVAH

Among observant Jews, the wedding marks the beginning of the observance of the laws of *Toharat Mishpacha* (family purity)[15]. As part of this, the bride (and sometimes the groom – separately) visits the *mikvah* (ritual *Bath*) prior to the wedding, usually the day before. The *mikvah* is used within Judaism to mark moments of change. In addition to brides and grooms, converts also immerse in the *mikvah* as part of the spiritual preparation of becoming a Jew and a *sofer* (scribe) will immerse prior to writing a Torah scroll.

The *mikvah* is a body of living water, *mayyim chayyim*. It is either a natural body of water or a collection of rain water, mixed with tap water. An indoor *mikvah* may look like a miniature swimming pool or spa. Jewish thought holds that all water comes from the river that left the Garden of Eden. According to the Talmud, the ultimate source of all water is the river that emerged from Eden. Immersion gives one a connection to the purity of Eden and fosters spiritual rebirth.

---

[15] *Toharat Mishpacha* (Family Purity) are the rules that govern contact between married couples during a woman's menstruation. It is considered a private observance between husband and wife. During her menstrual flow and the following seven days, the couple refrains from sexual contact. The women is in a state of *niddah* (separation). At the end of the following seven days, at night, the woman immerses in a *mikvah* and she and her husband are now permitted to engage intimate relations with each other. Observance of *Toharat Mishpacha* is governed by a series of *halachot*. For more information, see *A Guide to Jewish Religious Practice* by Rabbi Isaac Klein or consult your local rabbi.

Among Sephardim, going to the *mikvah* for the first time becomes an occasion of celebration. Some brides and grooms go to the *mikvah* with their closest friends.

A PRIVATE YOM KIPPUR

Yom Kippur is the holiest day of the Jewish calendar. It is a fast day on which each person reviews his or her past actions and does *teshuvah* (repentance) for the sins of the past year. For the bride and groom, the wedding day is considered to be a private Yom Kippur. On the day of the wedding, tradition has it that the couple's sins are forgiven, so that they can begin their new life together with a clean slate. On Yom Kippur, we dress the Torahs in white and the leaders of the synagogue will wear white because it represents purity. Therefore, the bride's gown is white. Some grooms will wear a white robe called a *kittel* over their suit or tuxedo during the ceremony. This robe is normally worn on Yom Kippur. Similarly, it is customary for the couple to fast until after the ceremony (except on certain special days, such as *Rosh Chodesh*).

KABBALAT PANIM

The wedding day is the bride and groom's opportunity to be queen and king for the day. Each will sit separately and welcome their guests during this period of *Kabbalat Panim* (literally greeting faces). Traditionally, the groom will hold a *chattan's tisch* (Yiddish for table) where he will joined by his friends and relatives. They will sing, tell stories, offer toasts, and study texts. The groom may be asked to give a d'var torah during which he will be frequently interrupted by his guests as they create a mood of joy and frivolity. Some couples also choose to have a *Kallah's tisch* for the bride.

KINYAN, KETUBAH AND BEDEKEN

Before the ceremony, there are two rituals which take place. Kinyan (acquisition) is a symbolic exchange, during which the groom is asked if he is prepared to fulfill his obligations as stated in the *ketubah* (wedding contract). The groom's acceptance of his obligations is expressed by his taking hold of a handkerchief given to him by the rabbi. This goes back to ancient times, when this act was the method by which agreements were considered binding. This act is done in the presence of the two witnesses who will sign the *ketubah*, immediately afterwards. These witnesses can not be related to each other, or to either the bride or the groom.

When bride and groom are finally prepared for the ceremony, they have a *Bedeken* (inspection or check). At the *Bedeken*, the groom covers the bride's face with the veil and may recite the following text:

וַיְבָרֲכוּ אֶת־רִבְקָה וַיֹּאמְרוּ לָהּ אֲחֹתֵנוּ אַתְּ הֲיִי לְאַלְפֵי רְבָבָה
וְיִירַשׁ זַרְעֵךְ אֵת שַׁעַר שֹׂנְאָיו:

And they blessed Rebekah, and said to her, You are our sister, be you the mother of thousands of ten thousands, and let your seed possess the gate of those who hate them.
(Bereishit 24:60)

This text was recited to Rebecca by her mother before she left her house to become Isaac's wife. The veil may have its origins in Rebecca's veiling of herself before meeting Isaac.

וַתֹּאמֶר אֶל־הָעֶבֶד
מִי־הָאִישׁ הַלָּזֶה הַהֹלֵךְ בַּשָּׂדֶה לִקְרָאתֵנוּ וַיֹּאמֶר הָעֶבֶד הוּא אֲדֹנִי וַתִּקַּח
הַצָּעִיף וַתִּתְכָּס:

And said to the servant, Who is that man walking in the field toward us? And the servant said,
that is my master. So she took her veil and covered herself. (Bereishit 24:65)

According to one interpretation, this ritual developed in order to prevent a recurrence of what happened to Jacob in the Bible. He was to marry Rachel, but her father tricked him by substituting Leah, Rachel's older sister, right before the ceremony. Also, lowering the veil over the bride's face represents an act of devotion between the couple.

After the veiling, the parents of the couple may offer blessings for them.

THE WEDDING CEREMONY סדר קידושין

Most weddings start with a processional. The custom of escorting bride and groom to the *huppah* is an old one. It symbolizes our comparison of them to king and queen. It is only fitting to escort "royalty" with an entourage. It is not necessary, from a Jewish standpoint, to have anyone "stand up" besides the couple and their parents. Best men, maids of honor, ushers, and bridesmaids are not required. In some communities, the guests rise as the bride and groom walk down the aisle.

The marriage ceremony consists of two parts which, originally, were separate events. *Erusin* or *Kiddushin* (betrothal) is the equivalent of engagement, and *Nissu'in* (marriage) is the equivalent of the actual wedding ceremony. In ancient times, the marriage was done in one of the following ways:

הָאִשָּׁה נִקְנֵית בְּשָׁלֹשׁ דְּרָכִים, וְקוֹנָה אֶת עַצְמָהּ בִּשְׁתֵּי דְרָכִים. נִקְנֵית בְּכֶסֶף, בִּשְׁטָר,
וּבְבִיאָה. בְּכֶסֶף, בֵּית שַׁמַּאי אוֹמְרִים, בְּדִינָר וּבְשָׁוֶה דִינָר. וּבֵית הִלֵּל אוֹמְרִים, בִּפְרוּטָה וּבְשָׁוֶה
פְרוּטָה. וְכַמָּה הִיא פְרוּטָה, אֶחָד מִשְּׁמוֹנָה בְּאִסָּר הָאִיטַלְקִי. וְקוֹנָה אֶת עַצְמָהּ בְּגֵט וּבְמִיתַת
הַבַּעַל. הַיְבָמָה נִקְנֵית בְּבִיאָה. וְקוֹנָה אֶת עַצְמָהּ בַּחֲלִיצָה וּבְמִיתַת הַיָּבָם:

A woman is acquired [in marriage] in three ways and acquires her herself in two ways. She is
acquired with money, with a document, or through marital relations. With money – the School of
Shammai says, with a dinar (a gold coin) or with the equivalent of a dinar; The School of Hillel
says, a perutah (a copper coin) or the worth of a perutah. And how much is a perutah? An eighth
of an Italian issar. (Mishna Kiddushin 1:1)

According to the text, what are the three ways that a marriage can occur?

The first method, "with money," is referred to as *kesef*. Originally, as stated in the text, actual coins were exchanged. Today, this concept has evolved into the transfer of a ring between the groom and the bride. The ring must be worth the equivalent of a *perutah* (the opinion of the School of Hillel). This is roughly equivalent to a penny.

The second method, "with a document," is called *Shtar*, literally contract. This is a written legal form which the groom hands over to the bride in front of at least two witnesses. The document included the details of the wedding (parties involved, date, place, etc.) as well as the formula, "Behold, you are consecrated..." (*Haray at Mekudeshet*...) The bride's acceptance of the *shtar* signified that the marriage had begun.

71

Marital relations, the last method, is referred to as *Bi'ah*. This form may seem surprising to us as a method of marriage, but in ancient times, the act of sex was a binding one, automatically resulting in marital status. Although the sources are somewhat confusing on this, it seems that there had to be intent to be married for the sex act to be binding. Intent would be signified by the recitation on the part of the male of the *"Haray at..."* formula.

Today, we allow only the first method, *kesef*.

When *Erusin* was separate from *Nissu'in*, it was still a binding relationship, not like engagement today. The couple was legally bound to each other, i.e., if either party had sex with a third person, it was considered adultery. Also, if either party decided to break off the relationship, the couple would have to undergo formal divorce proceedings. Thus, in Jewish legal tradition, the only difference between engagement and marriage was that the couple did not live together until *Nissu'in* (which could be a full year later). One of the reasons for the combination of *Erusin* and *Nissu'in* into this one ceremony is this very situation, which can be very frustrating—having all the responsibilities of married life, without one of the most obvious benefits, Another reason was historical necessity. Because of the precarious conditions under which Jews lived, there could never be any guarantee that a marriage would be completed.

In the present arrangement, the wedding ceremony combines both stages. The reading of the *Ketubah* (explained below) separates the two.

Jewish weddings are conducted underneath a *chuppah* (wedding canopy). This has various levels of symbolic meaning. One is that the canopy is a protecting cover, representing the knowledge that, as the couple joins in matrimony, they are protected from above, by God. It also symbolizes the home that the two will build together. Thirdly, it represents a carryover from ancient times, when bride and groom entered a wedding chamber, as part of the marriage ceremony, to consummate their marriage, while everyone waited anxiously outside. There are no qualifications for a *chuppah*, other than being large enough to cover the couple. Many families use a *tallit* for the *chuppah*, especially if it has sentimental value to the family (such as a grandfather's *taillit*).

ERUSIN/ KIDDUSHIN

When the bride reaches the *chupah*, it is traditional for her to circle the groom, either three or seven times. The mothers may guide the bride or hold her train as she circles. In some communities, the bride will circle the groom three times, then the groom will circle the bride three times. Then they will circle the inside of the *chupah* together to declare their ownership of this space.

A woman circles a man.

This custom is not an official part of the wedding ceremony, but it does hold meaning. During the Medieval Age, circles were considered protective and the bride creates a protected space for her groom.

Kiddushin officially begins with words of welcome to the bride, groom, and guests from the *M'sader Kiddushin* (the officiant). While it is not integral to a Jewish wedding to have a member of the clergy present, the *M'sader Kiddushin* is usually a rabbi or a cantor because of the dictates of the civil government (Clergy are allowed to sign marriage licenses.).

After the bridal party has entered, the *M'sader Kiddushin* begins.

בָּרוּךְ הַבָּא בשם יי!

May you who are here be blessed in The name of The Lord.

May He who is supreme in power, blessing and glory bless this bridegroom and this bride.

The *M'sader Kiddushin* may offer a brief prayer at this point.

Our tradition associates wine with joy. Thus, at all occasions of festivity and *simcha*, we partake of wine, with the appropriate blessing. During the ceremony, two cups are placed on a table under or near the *huppah*. One of the cups is used for the *Erusin* blessings, and the other is for the *Nissu'in* blessings. (At the wedding meal after the ceremony, when the seven wedding blessings are recited, wine from two cups is mixed. The bride and groom both drink from the mixed wine, symbolic of two separate lives becoming one.) A full cup of wine is held by the *M'sader Kiddushin* as he recites:

בָּרוּךְ אַתָּה יְיָ אֱלֹהֵינוּ מֶלֶךְ הָעוֹלָם, בּוֹרֵא פְּרִי הַגָּפֶן.

Blessed are you, Adonai our God, Ruler of the universe, who creates the fruit of the vine.

בָּרוּךְ אַתָּה יְיָ אֱלֹהֵינוּ מֶלֶךְ הָעוֹלָם, אֲשֶׁר קִדְּשָׁנוּ בְּמִצְוֹתָיו וְצִוָּנוּ עַל הָעֲרָיוֹת, וְאָסַר לָנוּ אֶת הָאֲרוּסוֹת, וְהִתִּיר לָנוּ אֶת הַנְּשׂוּאוֹת לָנוּ עַל יְדֵי חֻפָּה וְקִדּוּשִׁין. בָּרוּךְ אַתָּה יְיָ, מְקַדֵּשׁ עַמּוֹ יִשְׂרָאֵל עַל יְדֵי חֻפָּה וְקִדּוּשִׁין.

Praised are You, Adonai our God, who rules the universe, whose mitzvot add holiness to our lives and whose mitzvot will guide us even in the most intimate of our relationships. Praised are You, Adonai our God, who sanctifies the people Israel with Chupah, the wedding canopy, and Kiddushin, the sacred wedding traditions.

The cup of wine is presented first to the bridegroom and then to the bride.

The *M'sader Kiddushin* will say:

As you share the wine of this cup, so may you share all the things from this day on with love and with understanding.

The *M'sader Kiddushin* instructs the bridegroom to place the ring on the right forefinger of his bride and to say:

הֲרֵי אַתְּ מְקֻדֶּשֶׁת לִי, בְּטַבַּעַת זוּ כְּדַת מֹשֶׁה וְיִשְׂרָאֵל.

By this ring you arc consecrated to me as my wife in accordance with the Law of Moses and the people of Israel.

This ring must be a plain, round, usually golden ring. This was prescribed by tradition to prevent situations in which the bride may be tempted to accept a proposal of marriage primarily because of the ring offered to her. On a symbolic level, the ring, by virtue of its roundness and wholeness, represents eternity, which the couple will hopefully spend together. Many couples today have their rings engraved with a Hebrew, biblical phrase. Originally, only the bride received a ring. This stems from the concept of marriage as a legal transaction, and of in ancient times, only males had rights of ownership. Nowadays, many couples reflect the changed status of women by having a double-ring ceremony. The ring is placed on the index finger, since that finger is used to point with. Thus it can be clearly seen by the two witnesses who must watch the complete ceremony. (The ring can be switched to a different finger after the ceremony.)

A double ring ceremony can be part of a Jewish wedding with some stipulations. Most rabbis will insist upon a pause of some kind between the exchange of the rings. This is to ensure that it does not appear that the bride is returning the ring given to her by the groom and thus invalidating the marriage.

A bride might choose to recite something here such as

I am my beloved's and my beloved is mine

אני לדודי ודודי לי

Every legal procedure in Jewish life is confirmed by at least two witnesses. A Jewish wedding is a legal transaction between the bride and the groom. They make the ceremony binding upon the couple. The presence of witnesses makes a transitory moment permanent. It takes two witnesses (to the exclusion of others) to attest that the actions under the *chupah* have taken place in accordance with the laws of "Moses and Israel." Witnesses also sign the *ketubah* and keep watch at the door of the *yichud* room. Traditionally, witnesses are males who are over the age of thirteen and observant. These witnesses can under no circumstances be of the immediate family or even distant relatives to the participating parties.

KETUBAH-THE WEDDING CONTRACT

The reading of the *Ketubah* creates a break between the two parts of the wedding ceremony. The *Ketubah* is a legal document that states the interpersonal and financial obligations of the husband to his wife. Also included are the date and location of the ceremony and the bride and groom's names. The *ketubah* stipulates a cash settlement in the event of divorce to discourage the husband from frivolously divorcing his wife. The *Ketubah* is signed prior to the wedding ceremony by two witnesses who are not related to the couple (Some *ketubot* leave a space for the bride and groom to sign). This may strike you as decidedly unromantic and businesslike. The reason for this is to impress upon the couple the amount of responsibility and self-sacrifice that goes into being married.

The *ketubah* is traditionally written in Aramaic, which was the spoken language of the Jews in the Talmudic period. The text has gone through various stages of development throughout the centuries. Some *ketubot* are written in Hebrew or include English text. It is considered to be an evolution of the *shtar* (contract) method of marriage. The traditional text originates in Babylon. Originally it incorporated individual stipulations but it became standardized about 200 B.C.E. During the Gaonic period (mid-seventh to eleventh centuries), the Babylonian academies struggled for hegemony over their Palestinian counterparts. One of the results was the eradication of the Palestinian *ketubah* and the establishment of the standardized Babylonian *ketubah* in the practices of Jewish communities.

The Conservative Movement has added one paragraph to the text of the *ketubah*, often referred to as the Lieberman clause after its author, Professor Saul Lieberman. It names the Rabbinical Assembly as a Bet Din (Jewish Court); the couple agrees in advance that if either spouse demands a hearing before this court, the other will attend and accept its verdict. This was done in order to solve a serious legal problem. If a couple receives a divorce in a civil court and neglects to go through a Jewish *get* (divorce) proceeding, from the standpoint of Jewish Law the woman is still married. Thus if she remarries solely on the basis of a civil divorce, the second marriage is considered adultery, from the Jewish standpoint, and any children from that marriage would be considered *mamzerim* (children born from an illegal marriage).

A woman whose husband has refused to give her a *get* is called an *agunah* (chained woman). This has become a serious *halakhic* problem in Israel and North America. The Lieberman clause is an attempt to deal with this problem within a *halakhic* framework. The added paragraph gives the Rabbinical Assembly the power to enforce the laws of marriage and divorce, through the appropriate means. For this reason, a copy of the *ketubah* is generally sent to the Jewish Theological Seminary to be kept on file.

While there is some standardization for the text of the *ketubah*, there is none for the form. There is a concept in Jewish practice known as *Hiddur Mitzvah* (the beautification of a *mitzvah*). Whenever we have the means to go above and beyond the requirements of a law, we should do so. Hiring a calligrapher or artist to create a unique and original *ketubah* for a couple is an example of *hiddur mitzvah*. It is not necessary, but it is commendable.

SAMPLE KETUBAH—RABBINICAL ASSEMBLY TEXT 1987[16]

This translation of the new RA *Ketubah* (1987) was prepared by Rabbi Elliot Dorff.

We testify that on the day of _____week, the _____day of the month of _____in the year 57_____, corresponding to the _____day of _____, 20_____, here in _____, the groom, _____, said to the bride, _____, "Be my wife according to the laws and traditions of Moses and the Jewish people. I will work on your behalf and honor, sustain and support you according to the practice of Jewish men, who faithfully work on behalf of their wives and honor, sustain and support them. And I obligate myself to give you the sum of _____ zuzim as the money for your *Ketubah*, to which you are entitled (according to _____ law), and I will provide your food, clothing and necessities, and I will live with you in marital relations according to universal custom."

And the bride, _____, agreed to these and to become his wife, to participate together with him in establishing their home in love, harmony, peace and companionship according to the practice of Jewish women.

The groom, _____ accepted responsibility for the full dowry that she brought from her _____ house, whether in silver, gold, jewelry, clothes or furnishings, according to the sum of _____ zuzim, and agreed to increase the amount from his own assets with the sum of _____ zuzim, for a total of _____ zuzim.

The groom, _____, said "I take upon myself and my heirs after me the obligation of this *ketubah*, the dowry and the additional sum, to be paid from the best part of all my property, real and personal, that I now possess or may hereafter acquire. From this day forward, all my property, wherever it may be, even the mantle on my back, shall be mortgaged and liened for the payment of this *ketubah*, dowry, and additional sum, whether during my lifetime or thereafter." _____, the groom, took upon himself the obligations and strictures of this *ketubah*, this dowry and this additional sum as is customary with other ketubot made for Jewish women in accordance with the enactment of our Sages, may their memory be for a blessing. _____, the groom, and _____, the bride, further agreed that should either contemplate dissolution of their marriage, or following dissolution of their marriage in the civil courts each may summon the other to the Beit Din of the Rabbinical Assembly and the Jewish Theological Seminary of America, or its representative, and that each will abide by its instructions so that throughout life each will be able to live according to the laws of the Torah.

[16] Reprinted with permission from the Rabbinical Assembly.

This *Ketubah* is not to be regarded as mere rhetoric or as a perfunctory legal from. We have performed the act which in Jewish Law makes the obligations of this document legally binding on the part of _____, the groom, to _____, the bride, and on the part of _____, the bride, to _____, the groom, with an instrument fit for that purpose in order to confirm all that is stated and specified above, which shall be valid and immediately effective.

_____, Groom _____, Bride

_____, Witness _____, Witness

נוסח שטר כתובה

⁽¹⁾ _____ _____ בשבת _____ לחדש _____ ב

שנת חמשת אלפים ושבע מאות ⁽³⁾ _____ לבריאת העולם למנין שאנו מונין

כאן ⁽⁴⁾ _____ במדינת אמריקה הצפונית איך

החתן _____ בר _____ המכונה ⁽⁵⁾

אמר לה להדא ⁽⁶⁾ _____ _____

_____ המכונה ⁽⁵⁾ _____ בת

הוי לי לאנתו כדת משה וישראל ואנא אפלח ואוקיר ואיזון ואפרנס יתיכי ליכי

כהלכות גוברין יהודאין דפלחין ומוקרין וזנין ומפרנסין לנשיהון בקושטא ויהיבנא

ליכי ⁽⁷⁾ _____ _____ ומזוניכי וכסותיכי וספוקיכי ומיעל לותיכי כאורח

כל ארעא וצביאת מרת ⁽⁸⁾ _____ דא והות ליה לאנתו

לאשתתופי עמיה בצוותא לקיימא יבת ביתייהו באהבה ובאחוה בשלום וברעות

כמנהגא

דנשי יהודאן ודין נדוניא דהנעלת ליה מבי ⁽⁹⁾ _____ בין בכסף בין בדהב בין

בתכשיטין במאני דלבושא בשימושי דירה ובשימושי דערסא הכל קבל עליו _____

חתן דנן ⁽¹⁰⁾ _____ _____ זקוקים כסף צרוף וצבי

חתן דנן והוסיף לה מן דיליה עוד ⁽¹¹⁾ _____ _____ זקוקים כסף צרוף אחרים כנגדן

סך הכל ⁽¹²⁾ _____ _____ זקוקים כסף צרוף וכך אמר

חתן דנן אחריות שטר כתובתא דא נדוניא דין ותוספתא דא קבלית עלי ועל ירתי

בתראי להתפרע מן כל שפר ארג נכסין וקנינין דאית לי תחות כל שמיא דקנאי ודעתיד

אנא למקנא נכסין דאית להון אחריות ודלית להון אחריות כלהון יהון אחראין

וערבאין לפרוע מנהון שטר כתובתא דא נדוניא דין ותוספתא דא מנאי ואפילו מן

גלימא דעל כתפאי בחיי ובמותי מן יומא דנן ולעלם ואחריות וחומר שטר כתובתא

דא נדוניא דין ותוספתא דא קבל עליו _____ חתן דנן כחומר

כל שטרי כתובות ותוספתות דנהגין בבנות ישראל העשויין כתקון חכמינו זכרונם

לברכה. וצביאו מר _____ בר _____ ⁽⁵⁾ חתן דנן

ומרת _____ בת _____ ⁽⁵⁾ דאן יסיק

אדעתא דחד מינהון לנתוקי נישואיהון או אן איתנתוק נישואיהון בערכאות דמדינתא

דיכול דין או דא לזמנא לחבריה לבי דינא דכנישתא דרבנן ודבית מדרשא דרבנן

דארעתא דקיימא או מאן דאתי מן חילא וליצותו תרווייהו לפסקא דדיניה בדיל דיכלו

תרווייהו למיחי בדיני דאורייתא. דלא כאסמכתא ודלא כטפסי דשטרי. וקנינא מן

_____ בר _____ ⁽⁵⁾ חתן דנן למרת

_____ בת _____ ⁽⁵⁾ ומן מרת

_____ בת _____ ⁽⁵⁾ למר

_____ בר _____ ⁽⁵⁾ חתן דנן על

כל מה דכתוב ומפרש לעיל במנא דכשר למקנא ביה והכל שריר וקים.

נאום _____ עד

נאום _____ עד

77

Nisuin consist primarily of the recitation of the *Shevah Brachot* (Seven Blessings) which are recited over a second cup of wine. The latter six blessings originate from the Talmud (*Ketubot* 7b-8a) while the first is the blessing over the wine. Some couples choose to have the rabbi or cantor recite all of the blessings. Others choose to honor friends and family by having each blessing read by a different person.

בָּרוּךְ אַתָּה יְיָ אֱלֹהֵינוּ מֶלֶךְ הָעוֹלָם, בּוֹרֵא פְּרִי הַגָּפֶן.

Blessed are You, Adonai our God, Ruler of the universe, who creates the fruit of the vine.

בָּרוּךְ אַתָּה יְיָ אֱלֹהֵינוּ מֶלֶךְ הָעוֹלָם, שֶׁהַכֹּל בָּרָא לִכְבוֹדוֹ.

Praised are You, Adonai our God, Ruler of the universe, who created all things for Your glory.

בָּרוּךְ אַתָּה יְיָ אֱלֹהֵינוּ מֶלֶךְ הָעוֹלָם, יוֹצֵר הָאָדָם.

Praised are You, Adonai our God, Ruler of the universe, Creator of man.

בָּרוּךְ אַתָּה יְיָ אֱלֹהֵינוּ מֶלֶךְ הָעוֹלָם, אֲשֶׁר יָצַר אֶת הָאָדָם בְּצַלְמוֹ, בְּצֶלֶם דְּמוּת תַּבְנִיתוֹ, וְהִתְקִין לוֹ מִמֶּנּוּ בִּנְיַן עֲדֵי עַד. בָּרוּךְ אַתָּה יְיָ, יוֹצֵר הָאָדָם.

Praised are You, Adonai our God, Ruler of the universe, Who created man and woman in Your image, fashioning woman from man as his mate, that together they might perpetuate life. Praised are You, Adonai, Creator of man.

שׂוֹשׂ תָּשִׂישׂ וְתָגֵל הָעֲקָרָה בְּקִבּוּץ בָּנֶיהָ לְתוֹכָהּ בְּשִׂמְחָה. בָּרוּךְ אַתָּה יְיָ, מְשַׂמֵּחַ צִיּוֹן בְּבָנֶיהָ.

May Zion rejoice as her children are restored to her in joy. Praised are You, Adonai, who causes Zion to rejoice at her children's return.

שַׂמֵּחַ תְּשַׂמַּח רֵעִים הָאֲהוּבִים כְּשַׂמֵּחֲךָ יְצִירְךָ בְּגַן עֵדֶן מִקֶּדֶם. בָּרוּךְ אַתָּה יְיָ, מְשַׂמֵּחַ חָתָן וְכַלָּה.

Grant perfect joy to these loving companions, as You did to the first man and woman in the Garden of Eden. Praised are You, Adonai, Who grants the joy of the bride and groom.

בָּרוּךְ אַתָּה יְיָ אֱלֹהֵינוּ מֶלֶךְ הָעוֹלָם, אֲשֶׁר בָּרָא שָׂשׂוֹן וְשִׂמְחָה, חָתָן וְכַלָּה, גִּילָה, רִנָּה, דִּיצָה וְחֶדְוָה, אַהֲבָה וְאַחֲוָה וְשָׁלוֹם וְרֵעוּת. מְהֵרָה יְיָ אֱלֹהֵינוּ יִשָּׁמַע בְּעָרֵי יְהוּדָה וּבְחֻצוֹת יְרוּשָׁלַיִם קוֹל שָׂשׂוֹן וְקוֹל שִׂמְחָה, קוֹל חָתָן וְקוֹל כַּלָּה, קוֹל מִצְהֲלוֹת חֲתָנִים מֵחֻפָּתָם וּנְעָרִים מִמִּשְׁתֵּה נְגִינָתָם. בָּרוּךְ אַתָּה יְיָ, מְשַׂמֵּחַ חָתָן עִם הַכַּלָּה.

Praised are You, Adonai our God, Ruler of the universe, who created joy and gladness, bride and groom, mirth, song, delight and rejoicing, love and harmony, peace and companionship. Adonai, may there ever be heard in the cities of Judah and in the streets of Jerusalem voices of joy and gladness, voices of bride and groom, the jubilant voices of those joined in marriage under the bridal canopy, the voices of young people feasting and singing. Praised are You, Adonai, who causes the groom to rejoice with his bride.

The *M'sader Kiddushin* may choose to end by pronouncing the couple married or by offering them one of the following blessings:

1. *May you be blessed with joy and gladness, vigor of body and spirit, love and harmony, companionship and peace.*

2. *May God bless you and keep you*

    יְבָרֶכְךָ יְיָ וְיִשְׁמְרֶךָ:

    May God be with you and be gracious unto you.

    יָאֵר יְיָ פָּנָיו אֵלֶיךָ וִיחֻנֶּךָּ:

    May God show you kindness and give you peace.

    יִשָּׂא יְיָ פָּנָיו אֵלֶיךָ וְיָשֵׂם לְךָ שָׁלוֹם:
    Numbers 6:24-26

MAZEL TOV!

At the end of the ceremony, the groom breaks a glass with his foot. There are various interpretations of the symbolic meaning of this act. The most well-known one is that it represents the destruction of the Temple. This reminds us that even at times of greatest joy and happiness, we should not forget the suffering of our people, past and present. A second interpretation is that just as the breaking of the glass is permanent and irrevocable, so too should be the marriage of the couple.

YICHUD

Following the ceremony, it is customary for the couple to enter a private room for a few moments. This ritual is called *Yihud* (unification). Originally, this had one function—the consummation of the marriage which, as mentioned earlier, is one of the ways that a marriage could occur (*bi'ah*). Today, this is simply a time for the couple to take a breather and to break their fast, together.

SEUDAT *MITZVAH*

A *Seudat Mitzvah* celebrates the *mitzvah* of getting married. Typically, music and dancing are part of the meal. Entertainment has been an important part of the wedding celebration since Talmudic times.

> They tell of R. Judah b. Ila'i that he used to take a myrtle twig and dance before the bride and say: 'Beautiful and graceful bride.' R. Samuel the son of R. Isaac danced with three [twigs]. That is some things they did to entertain the bride. And also R. Aha took her on his shoulder and danced [with her]. The Rabbis said to him: May we [also] do it? He said to them: If they are on you like a beam, [then it is] all right. And if not, [you may] not. (Babylonian Talmud, Ketubot 17a)

Have you ever been to a wedding party? What goes on?

Do the rabbi's actions sound entertaining? How would you entertain the bride and groom at their wedding?

The meal concludes with the recitation of *Birkat HaMazon* (Blessing after a Meal). Included as part of it are the *Sheva Brachot* recited during *Nisuin*. Two cups of wine are poured. The first is held by the person leading *Birkat HaMazon*. The other cup is passed around to each of the people saying one of the *Sheva Brachot*. When recited with *Birkat HaMazon*, the blessing over wine is recited last.

The celebration of the wedding continues for seven days after the wedding. At each meal where the couple is present, along with a minyan and a new guest, the *Sheva Brachot* are recited. This is a way to extend the joy of the celebration of the wedding to those who were not at the wedding.

 **Every couple who gets married chooses a different aspect of the ceremony to focus on with something special or creative.**

Which of the wedding ceremonies you just studied would you emphasize at your wedding? Why?

How is the Jewish Wedding Ceremony…

A Cause For Rejoicing	Something that tied me to tradition	Something that made me feel important	Something that helps Jewish unity

DAYS WHEN MARRIAGES MAY NOT BE PERFORMED

1. *Shabbat* and Festivals—the principle here is that the joy (*simha*) of observing *Shabbat* and Festivals should not be compromised or shared by another *simha*. This probably stems from our tragedy-filled history, which created a desire to cherish every possible occasion for rejoicing and celebration. A second reason is that legally, marriage is considered to be a form of business, and this is prohibited on *Shabbat* and Holidays. On the other hand, a marriage may not take place on a day of mourning.

2. The first nine days of the month of Av -these days are considered a period of national mourning, since according to tradition, this period marks the final stages in the conquest of Jerusalem and the destruction of both the First (586 B.C.E.) and Second (70 C.E.) Temples. Some Jews will

avoid weddings as early as the 17th of the previous month (Tammuz), since that day commemorates the crumbling of the walls around Jerusalem.

3. The 49 days of the Omer - there are 49 days between Passover and *Shavuot* which are counted each night. This is referred to as *Sefirat HaOmer* (counting of the *omer*). This originally stems from the agricultural needs of the people to know when to harvest certain crops. Later, the period became one of mourning, due to a plague that was alleged to have broken out among a large number of rabbinical students. In some circles, weddings will not take place during this entire time, with the exception of *Lag B'Omer*—the 33rd day of the Omer (according to the legend, the plague lifted for this one day), and *Rosh Chodesh* (both Iyar and Sivan take place during this period). The position of the Conservative Movement is presently to avoid weddings between Passover and Yom *HaShoah* (Holocaust Day, the 27th of Nisan. Still others allow weddings on *Yom Ha'Atzmaut* (Israel Independence Day, the 5th of Iyar).

Discussion

1. **Discuss the pros and cons of matchmaking.**

2. **If you were "designing" a wedding ceremony, what would it include? Compare your ideas to the traditional ceremony.**

CREATING YOUR WEDDING

Create your wedding program--Due to how many different traditions there are at a Jewish wedding, many couples choose to write up a short guide to their wedding. Create your own guide to a wedding, complete with your own interpretation of the traditions, or use one the ideas in this sourcebook.

PART OF WEDDING	MY PLAN
AUFRUF	*How might you organize your Aufruf? Will both you and your future spouse be called to the Torah?*
KETUBAH	*What type of Ketubah would you like?*
TANAIM	*Would you have this ceremony? How might you make it special?*

BEDEKEN	*Would you hold this ceremony in public or private? Would you add any personal prayers?*
CHUPAH	*Who might you ask to participate in this part of the ceremony?*
SHEVA BRACHOT	*Who might you invite to recite the brachot?*

elderly and aging

HONORING THE ELDERLY הִדּוּר פְּנֵי זָקֵן

The prosperity of a country is in accordance with the treatment of the aged.

Rabbi Nachman of Braslov

There are no specific life cycle events tied to growing older. Judaism does not mark a midlife crisis with a ceremony. Rather, as you age life is filled with coordinating and attending the life cycle events of your children, friends, and relatives. Judaism, however, does not ignore the aging process. Rather, a strong tradition of hiddur p'nai zaken (honoring the elderly) exists.

WHAT IS THE JEWISH TRADITION OF HIDDUR P'NAI *ZAKEN*?[17]

אַל־תַּשְׁלִיכֵנִי לְעֵת זִקְנָה כִּכְלוֹת כֹּחִי אַל־תַּעַזְבֵנִי:

Do not cast me off in old age; when my strength fails, do not forsake me! (Tehillim 71:9)

This prayer, recited especially on Yom Kippur, is addressed not to man, but to God; it is a plea that can also be answered through fulfillment by other Jews of their moral obligations to honor their parents and to care for those in need of help.

1. **Why do you think that this prayer is recited on Yom Kippur?**

2. **What connection does it have with Yom Kippur?**

והזהרו בזקן ששכח תלמודו מחמת אונסו' דאמרינן: לוחות ושברי לוחות מונחות בארון.

Even the old man who has forgotten his learning must be treated tenderly, for were not the broken tablets placed in the Ark of the Covenant side by side with the whole ones? (Brachot 8b)

---

[17] Chapter excerpted from Barbara Fortgang Summers/ Dara Zabb: *Tzorchei Tzibbur: Community and Responsibility*. United Synagogue Youth, 1999.

The verse quoted above from the Talmud refers to the story in the Torah when Moses first smashes the Ten Commandments after seeing that the Israelites built the Golden Calf. When he gets a second set of tablets, both the whole tablets and the smashed ones are placed in the ark of the Covenant.

Why do you think that is? What does that say about us as human beings?

DEFINING ELDERLY: PERSPECTIVES ON HIDDUR P'NAI *ZAKEN*

Read the following text from *Vayikra* 19:32. What does the text instruct us to do? Why do you think it gives these instructions?

מִפְּנֵי שֵׂיבָה תָּקוּם וְהָדַרְתָּ פְּנֵי זָקֵן וְיָרֵאתָ מֵאֱלֹהֶיךָ אֲנִי יְהֹוָה:

*You shall rise before the aged (*seva*) and show deference to the old (*zaken*); You shall fear your God: I am Adonai. (Vayikra 19:32)*

1. **Does it make sense for us today to rise before the old?**

2. **If we did, what would we be saying about our attitudes toward the elderly?**

3. **Do you think that there is a difference between the old (*zaken*) and the aged (*sevah*)?**

4. **How do the two parts of the sentence fit together?**

5. **What connection could there be between honoring an old man and fearing God?**

הוּא הָיָה אוֹמֵר, בֶּן חָמֵשׁ שָׁנִים לַמִּקְרָא, בֶּן עֶשֶׂר לַמִּשְׁנָה, בֶּן שְׁלֹשׁ עֶשְׂרֵה לַמִּצְוֹת, בֶּן חֲמֵשׁ עֶשְׂרֵה לַתַּלְמוּד, בֶּן שְׁמוֹנֶה עֶשְׂרֵה לַחֻפָּה, בֶּן עֶשְׂרִים לִרְדּוֹף, בֶּן שְׁלֹשִׁים לַכֹּחַ, בֶּן אַרְבָּעִים לַבִּינָה, בֶּן חֲמִשִּׁים לָעֵצָה, בֶּן שִׁשִּׁים לַזִּקְנָה, בֶּן שִׁבְעִים לַשֵּׂיבָה, בֶּן שְׁמוֹנִים לַגְּבוּרָה, בֶּן תִּשְׁעִים לָשׁוּחַ, בֶּן מֵאָה כְּאִלּוּ מֵת וְעָבַר וּבָטֵל מִן הָעוֹלָם:

*He [Judah ben Tema] used to say: "At five years of age—the study of Bible, at ten—the study of Mishnah, at thirteen—responsibility for the mizvot, at fifteen—the study of Talmud, at eighteen—marriage, at twenty—pursuit of a livelihood, at thirty—the peak of one's powers, at forty—the age of understanding, at fifty—the age of counsel, at sixty –old age (*ziknah*), at seventy –white old age (*sevah*), at eighty—the age of "strength," at ninety—the bent back, at one hundred –as one dead and gone from the world. (Avot 5:23)*

According to this text, what is the difference between *ziknah* and *sevah*?

We now have an insight into the Jewish attitude towards the aged; a *zaken* is deserving of honor no matter what his scholarly accomplishments have been. As much as we are to show respect for one who has acquired Torah, an old man is to be honored even if he has not acquired knowledge of the Torah. But why should this be so? When we honor one who has acquired much knowledge of the Torah, it is not the person himself we are honoring, but rather the Torah that he embodies.

1. **Why then must we honor the physical presence of the** *zaken*?

2. **What is there about a** *zaken* **that commands the respect that we are supposed to show him?**

HIDDUR P'NAI *ZAKEN*

Then...

Before answering these questions, it is necessary that we reflect upon the way in which *zekenim* were treated in Talmudic and Medieval times. In the first place, there simply were not many people alive in any one generation who reached what we would call "old age." Life expectancy was perhaps 40 or 50 years at most. It was unusual for one to live to the age of *zikna* (defined in the Talmud as being a minimum of 60 years). People looked up to the aged in the hope that they too would be blessed with such a long life. Who, indeed, would not have stood in awe as a person who had reached the age of *zikna* (60) or *seva* (70) entered a room! In traditional societies respect for elders was a virtue inculcated into children from infancy. Bestowing honor on elders (*zekenim* as well as parents) was a commandment that needed little rationale from Maimonides' time until modern times.

And now...

In modern society respect for the aged does not come quite so automatically. It is no longer unusual for a person to be alive and mobile at the age of 80 or even 90. The achievement of age no longer possesses the almost mystical aura that it once had. Moreover, old people at the ages of *zikna* and *seva* are far more common now than ever before. Perhaps modern people have become desensitized to the wonder of old age. We take old age for granted: it is no longer a goal to pray for, but an inevitability to be postponed for as long as possible.

Today people age 70 and up are living rich, full lives. The internet, telephones and e-mail all help to allow even those people who are homebound to keep up with the outside world on a moment-to-moment basis.

ACTIVITY: DEFINING ELDERLY

List the names of some elderly people with whom you are acquainted. Briefly describe them—how they look, what they do, etc.

1. Name_____ Age_____

Relationship to you_____Description_____

_____

_____

2. Name_____ Age_____

Relationship to you_____Description_____

_____

_____

1. **How many of your elderly acquaintances are over 70?**

2. **Do you consider people over 60 to be elderly? Are your grandparents elderly?**

It used to be that people did not live as long on the average as we do today. A person who was fortunate to live to be 60 or 70 was quite a rarity.

3. **Do we consider it unusual for people to live to be 60 or 70?**

4. **What is an age we might consider to be unusually old?**

5. **How should we define the group of people we call "elderly"?**

The rather arbitrary grouping "over 65" includes the widest variety of people. There are the "young" elderly—a great many of whom work, do extensive volunteer service, travel and live as actively as when they were "young"—and there are the physically infirm who cannot work or move around easily, and who are often isolated in their homes or confined to nursing homes. As with any other age group, there is a wide diversity in health, education, housing, income, religious attitudes and behavior, mental outlook, family status, and geographical location.

Respect for the elderly that we learn from *Vayikra* 19:32 teaches us the idea to "Honor your mother and father."

1. **How might these two ideas be related? In earlier times, when people died at earlier ages, old age came on at a relatively earlier time than today.**

2. **Do you consider your parents to be elderly?**

3. **How is the respect that you give to your parents different from the respect demanded in *Vayikra* for the elderly? How is it the same?**

4. **What do you think are the characteristics of being parents and of being old that are the same?**

HIDDUR P'NAI *ZAKEN* IN NORTH AMERICAN HISTORY

It is clear from the early history of the synagogue that it has been a unique institution – it served as the hub of the community, and the focus for carrying out the mitzvot enumerated in the Mishnah Peah excerpted above. Special groups were organized through the synagogue with such titles as "Upbringers of Orphans," "Clothers of the Naked," "Crown of the Aged," "Comforters of Mourners" and so on. There were voluntary associations of lay persons whose participation was inspired both by the Law and their association with the synagogue-community. In the middle ages, the elderly in need of care may have been cared for in shelters for the sick or in places for the homeless (hekdesh). The need for treating the aged as a separate group apart from the sick and the poor did not come until modern times, as industrialization and urbanization disrupted and estranged families. Societies for the aging and homes for the aged grew up during the nineteenth century and, in America, proliferated with the massive Eastern European migration—and the resultant disruptions of family life.

The sponsorship of philanthropy also came from many concerned, non-observant Jews, and thus many of the social services established for new immigrants and the aged were organized by Jews out of a traditional notion of obligation, but without direct reference to either the Law or the synagogue. Urbanization encouraged the centralization of aged care, and the professionalization of social work contributed to the separation of the synagogue and social service agencies. By 1930, the separation was virtually complete. Prior to 1900, there were only nine Jewish homes for the aged; today there are homes in virtually every major Jewish community.

As a result of the centralization, professionalization and transience of modern American society, the synagogue has been weakened as an institution. The requirements of centralization not only of social services, but of fund-raising and education, have lessened reliance on the synagogue for providing community leadership; the professionalization of life, including the functions within the synagogue, have lessened attendance and participation in the regular observances of Judaism; and transience which restricts the time and motivation to sink roots has attenuated loyalties between families and local institutions. These trends have radically altered the societal framework and the attitudinal structure through which the modern Jew deals with his aging relatives and with his own aging process. Ironically, these societal trends have in turn increased the consciousness of a need for stronger local institutions and thus a greater role in the local synagogue. [18]

As much as synagogues and communities today have a renewed responsibility toward the elderly, so too must each individual undertake action to help the aged.

---

[18] A Guide to Aging Programs for Synagogues, New York: The Synagogue Council of America, 1975, pp. 9-10

What role can you play in taking responsibility toward the elderly?

The needs of the elderly are constantly changed by the multiple losses of role, status, income and health. They are further affected by the loss of spouse, family, neighbors and friends through death or migration. An older person may find himself isolated at a time when the emotional support of others is needed. Fear, loneliness and enforced inactivity reduce participation in community life and increase isolation. Caught in this cycle, and unaware of existing community services which are available to help, these people are the most difficult to identify and often the neediest.

ACTIVITY: Understanding the Needs of the Elderly

What are some needs and desires of the elderly people that you mentioned in the activity "Defining Elderly"?

1.

2.

3.

4.

5.

1. **Which of these needs can be satisfied by individuals like you? How?**

2. **Which of these needs can be satisfied by the Jewish community? How?**

3. **Which of these needs may not be able to be satisfied at all? Why?**

4. **Where are there places in your individual communities where you think that you might be able to make a difference with the elderly?**

TRADITION TEACHES US ABOUT OLD AGE

In Jewish tradition it is not only said that we must honor our elders, but that it is an honor to achieve a ripe old age. Advanced years in themselves are not an honor, but when achieved "in the way of righteousness," then they are considered to be wearing "a crown of glory." (*Mishlei* 16:31).

The Bible emphasizes the inter-relationship between the way in which we live our lives, and the nature of the "harvest" of old age. The Fifth Commandment states: "Honor your father and mother, which your days may be long in the land that the Lord your God gives to you." The belief that longevity is the reward for a good life is summed up in Jacob's response to the Pharoah's question asking Jacob's age. He answered:

וַיֹּאמֶר יַעֲקֹב אֶל־פַּרְעֹה יְמֵי שְׁנֵי מְגוּרַי שְׁלֹשִׁים וּמְאַת שָׁנָה מְעַט וְרָעִים הָיוּ יְמֵי שְׁנֵי חַיַּי וְלֹא הִשִּׂיגוּ אֶת־יְמֵי שְׁנֵי חַיֵּי אֲבֹתַי בִּימֵי מְגוּרֵיהֶם:

The days of the years of my sojournings are a hundred and thirty years; few and evil have been the days of the years of my life, and they have not attained unto the days of the years of the life of my fathers in the days of their sojournings. (Bereshit 47:9)

The rabbinic literature offers a poignant counterpoint between the growth in wisdom and learning that is achievable only with age, and the physical decline characteristic of old age.

"He who learns from the young eats unripe grapes and drinks new wine," it is stated in the Talmud; while "he who learns from the old eats ripe grapes and drinks old wine." Another rabbinic sage advised: "If the old say 'tear down' and the children 'build' – then you should tear down, for the 'destruction' of the old is 'construction;' the 'construction' of the young, 'destruction.'" As for the physical realities, the unattractiveness of old age is treated metaphorically: "Youth is a crown of roses; old age a crown of (heavy) willows;" and practically: a man must pray that in his later years, "his eyes may see, his mouth eat, his legs walk, for in old age all powers fail."

According to the rabbis too, age itself is not a virtue; wisdom and knowledge of Torah determine its value. The truly successful life is one which goes on growing and developing to the very end, which reaches its last day with full mental and physical powers. (*D'varim.* 34:7). [19]

וְאַתָּה תָּבוֹא אֶל־אֲבֹתֶיךָ בְּשָׁלוֹם תִּקָּבֵר בְּשֵׂיבָה טוֹבָה:

(God said to Abram), "You shall go to your fathers in peace; you shall be buried at a ripe old age." (Bereshit 15:15)

לֹא־יִהְיֶה מִשָּׁם עוֹד עוּל יָמִים וְזָקֵן אֲשֶׁר לֹא־יְמַלֵּא אֶת־יָמָיו כִּי הַנַּעַר בֶּן־מֵאָה שָׁנָה יָמוּת וְהַחוֹטֶא בֶּן־מֵאָה שָׁנָה יְקֻלָּל:

No more shall there be an infant or a graybeard who does not live out his days. He who dies at a hundred years shall be reckoned a youth, and he who failed to reach a hundred shall be reckoned accursed. (Isaiah 65:20)

כַּבֵּד אֶת־אָבִיךָ וְאֶת־אִמֶּךָ לְמַעַן יַאֲרִכוּן יָמֶיךָ עַל הָאֲדָמָה אֲשֶׁר־יְהוָֹה אֱלֹהֶיךָ נֹתֵן לָךְ:

Honor your father and mother that your days may be long upon the land that the Lord your God gives you. (Shemot 20:12)

---

[19] *A Guide to Aging Programs for Synagogues, pp. 5-9*

Compare this verse from *Shemot* 20:12 to the verse in *Vayikra* 19:32 found near the beginning of this chapter. Are the two related?

CONTRASTING TEXTS

Read the following texts and consider what they mean to you.

בִּישִׁישִׁים חָכְמָה וְאֹרֶךְ יָמִים תְּבוּנָה:

With aged men is wisdom; And length of day brings understanding. (Job 12:12)

לֹא־רַבִּים יֶחְכָּמוּ וּזְקֵנִים יָבִינוּ מִשְׁפָּט:

The old are not always wise; Nor do the aged understand judgment. (Job 32:9)

1. **How could the author of the Book of Job believe in both of these ideas? Don't they contradict one another?**

אין מושיבין בסנהדרי אלא בעלי קומה' ובעלי חכמה' ובעלי מראה' ובעלי זקנה'

None are to be appointed members of the Sanhedrin but men of stature, wisdom, good appearance, mature age… (Sanhedrin 17a)

2. **Why is each one of these things important?**

3. **What if a person has some qualities, but not the others?**

אין מושיבין בסנהדרין זקן וסריס ומי שאין לו בנים רבי יהודה מוסיף: אף אכזרי.

We do not appoint as members of the Sanhedrin an aged man, a eunuch, or one who is childless. Rabbi Judah added: a cruel man. (Sanhedrin 36b)

4. **Don't these two verses also contradict each other?**

5. **How can the two descriptions of the Sanhedrin members both be in the Talmud?**

6. **How might each verse refer to different situations or circumstances?**

7. **Why does Jewish tradition have differing opinions toward treatment of the elderly?**

We now have an insight into the Jewish attitude towards the aged; a *zaken* is deserving of honor no matter what his scholarly accomplishments have been. As much as we are to show respect for one who has acquired Torah, an old man is to be honored even if he has not acquired knowledge of the Torah. But why should this be so? When we honor one who has acquired much knowledge of the Torah, it is not the person himself we are honoring, but rather the Torah that he embodies.

8. **Why then must we honor the physical presence of the *zaken*?**

9. **What is there about a *zaken* that commands the respect that we are supposed to show him?**

Now read the next two texts from *Kiddishin* and *Sefer HaChinuch* and think about the following questions:

1. **What do the elderly possess that should entitle them to the respect of younger people?**

2. **Do you agree with Issi ben Yehuda when he says that we should rise before the aged, regardless of whether or not they are learned in the Torah?**

3. **What do all elderly people have, according to Issi ben Yehuda?**

ת"ר: (ויקרא יט) מפני שיבה תקום – יכול אפילו מפני זקן
אשמאי? ת"ל: זקן ואין זקן אלא חכם' שנאמר: (במדבר יא) אספה לי
שבעים איש מזקני ישראל – רבי יוסי הגלילי אומר: אין זקן אלא מי שקנה חכמה'
שנאמר: (משלי ח) ה, קנני ראשית דרכו.
איסי בן יהודה אומר: מפני שיבה תקום – אפילו כל שיבה במשמע.

Our Rabbis taught: "You shall rise before the aged and show deference to the old; you shall fear your God: I am the Lord" (Vayikra 19:32). You might think one must honor even a wicked old man. But the Torah used the word zaken (elder) which means "wise man", as it says, "Gather for Me seventy men from the elders of Israel, whom you know to be elders and officers of the people, and bring them to the Tent of Meeting and let them take their place with you" (Bamidbar 11:16). [In this sense, elders take on a connotation of more than just "old men".] R. Yose the Galilean says zaken (an 'elder') is only one who acquired wisdom, as it says, "The Lord made me (kanani) as the beginning of His way" [Proverb 8:22 – based on a play on the Hebrew word "kanani"] ...Issi ben Yehuda says, "You shall rise before the aged. This means that all old men (whether they are wise or not) are included." (Kiddushin 32b)

4. **Does this mean that elders are always right?**

5. **What is the text trying to teach regarding the relationship of elders and young people?**

Honor of the wise:

One of the rationales for this mitzvah is that the essence of man in this world is to acquire more and more wisdom in order to know his Creator. Therefore it is fitting to honor one who has attained wisdom, so that others will be encouraged to do the same. And for this reason, Issi ben Yehuda said in the Gemara (Kiddushin 32b) that even a wicked old man [deserves honor]. That is, one who is not knowledgeable is included in the mitzvah of honoring the elderly, since during his many years he has come to recognize God's works and His wonders, and therefore he (the zaken) should be honored. And this agrees with what R. Yohanan said, that the law is according to Issi ben Yehuda; "As long as the old person is not a blatant sinner; because if so, he prevents himself from being honored." (Sefer HaHinuch, No. 257)

6. **What does this selection from Sefer HaChinuch add to the text from the Talmud in Kiddushin 32b?**

7. **Does anything we have read in Job or Sanhedrin modify in any way the ideas found in *Vayikra*, *Kiddushin* or *Sefer HaChinuch*—that the elderly deserve respect because they are wise in their own experience?**

…when they can no longer work?

וַיְדַבֵּר יְהוָה אֶל־מֹשֶׁה לֵּאמֹר:
זֹאת אֲשֶׁר לַלְוִיִּם מִבֶּן חָמֵשׁ וְעֶשְׂרִים שָׁנָה וָמַעְלָה יָבוֹא לִצְבֹא צָבָא
בַּעֲבֹדַת אֹהֶל מוֹעֵד: וּמִבֶּן חֲמִשִּׁים שָׁנָה יָשׁוּב מִצְּבָא הָעֲבֹדָה וְלֹא יַעֲבֹד
עוֹד: וְשֵׁרֵת אֶת־אֶחָיו בְּאֹהֶל מוֹעֵד לִשְׁמֹר מִשְׁמֶרֶת וַעֲבֹדָה לֹא יַעֲבֹד
כָּכָה תַּעֲשֶׂה לַלְוִיִּם בְּמִשְׁמְרֹתָם:

The Lord spoke to Moses saying, "This is the rule for the Levites; from 25 years of age up
they shall participate in the work force in the service of the Tent of Meeting but at age 50 they
shall retire from the work force and shall serve no more. They may assist their brother Levites
at the Tent of Meeting by standing guard, but they shall perform no labor. Thus you shall deal
with the Levites with regard to their duties." (Bemidbar 8:23-26)

…when they are physically weak and cannot take care of themselves?

אַל־תַּשְׁלִיכֵנִי לְעֵת זִקְנָה כִּכְלוֹת כֹּחִי אַל־תַּעַזְבֵנִי:

Do not cast me off in time of old age; Forsake me not when my strength is spent. (Tehillim 71:9)

צריך אדם להתפלל על זקנתו שתהא עיניו רואות
ופיו אוכל ורגליו מהלכות שבזמן שאדם יזקין הכל מסתלק ממנו

A person must pray concerning his old age that his eyes see, his mouth eat, and his legs walk,
for in old age these abilities depart. (Tanhuma, Mikketz 10)

…when they are mentally incapacitated and are easily confused and forgetful?

והלומד זקן למה הוא דומה. לדיו כתובה על ניר מחוק.

What does learning when old resemble? It is like writing on blotted paper. (Avot 4:25)

…when they are defenseless against the cruelty of others?

וְנִגַּשׂ הָעָם אִישׁ בְּאִישׁ וְאִישׁ בְּרֵעֵהוּ יִרְהֲבוּ הַנַּעַר בַּזָּקֵן וְהַנִּקְלֶה בַּנִּכְבָּד:

So the people shall oppress one another—Each oppressing his fellow: The young shall bully
the old, and the despised shall bully the honored. (Isaiah 3:5)

…when they fear the end of life and the insecurities of the future?

שְׂמַח בָּחוּר בְּיַלְדוּתֶיךָ וִיטִיבְךָ לִבְּךָ בִּימֵי בְחוּרוֹתֶךָ וְהַלֵּךְ בְּדַרְכֵי
לִבְּךָ וּבְמַרְאֵי עֵינֶיךָ וְדָע כִּי עַל־כָּל־אֵלֶּה יְבִיאֲךָ הָאֱלֹהִים בַּמִּשְׁפָּט:

Rejoice, O young man, in your youth, and be happy in the days of your youth, and walk in the ways of your heart, and in the sight of your eyes… (Kohelet 11:9)

כשאדם נער אומר דברי זמר' הגדיל אומר דברי משלות' הזקין אומר דברי הבלים.

When a man is young he quotes poetry; when he matures, he quotes proverbs; when he is old, he speaks of futilities. (Shir HaShirim Rabbah 1:10)

We can now try to understand why any *zaken* is deserving of honor.

HOW DO WE ANSWER THESE QUESTIONS?

1. Today, there are more opportunities for the elderly then ever before. What are some things that you do, which you think that elderly people can not do?

2. Should age be a hindrance for someone who wants to skydive, to play basketball, or to work in a full time position?

A NEW CHALLENGE: ALZHEIMER'S DISEASE

Alzheimer's is a disease that primarily affects the elderly and causes the loss of basic memory functions.

1. How do you think it would feel to visit a close relative who no longer recognizes you?

2. Does your visit matter if they won't remember that you were there?

TREATMENT OF THE DYING

While death is inevitable, life is sacred and must be preserved as long as possible; the sick must be comforted and healed. It is, in fact, a *mitzvah* (not only a good deed, but also a religious command and obligation) to visit the sick (*bikur cholim*). Since it is the comfort of the patient that is sought, the Rabbis have given detailed instructions when and how to visit the sick, what to do and what not to do at these visits. In some cases, they even permit someone to violate the Sabbath in order to take care of someone who is sick. Despite the importance of the act, the Rabbis also warned that visits made at an inappropriate time, or lasting too long, may make the patient uncomfortable and should therefore be avoided. The visitor should be guided by the attending doctor or nurse, and by his own common sense. [20]

As with so many mitzvot, the Jewish community did not leave matters entirely to the benevolence and piety of the individual. Every community had a Bikkur Holim Society, first mentioned by Rabbi Nissim Girondi (1360). Before the days of hospitals, these societies did

---

[20] Adapted from A Time to Be Born A Time to Die, By Rabbi Isaac Klein, United Synagogue Youth, 1988.

not limit their work to mere visiting. They also relieved the exhausted family members of attending to the needs of the sick, and often helped financially, too, when the patient was the breadwinner of the family.

In our day, these commendable acts have been relegated to the rabbi and the religious functionaries of the synagogue. This has the virtues of our age of specialization in that the rabbi usually knows what to do in varied situations, and that the position of the rabbi and the confidence the patient generally has in him are a great comfort. Nevertheless, the traditional requirement that the obligation fell upon everyone is preferred, and should be encouraged. In this regard, Bikkur Holim can be an important and rewarding USY chapter project.

Even more important than visiting the ill, however, is the supreme obligation to preserve life as long as it is possible. Thus, the classical text tells us:

> *A dying man is considered the same as a living man in every respect.*
>
> *His jaws may not be bound, nor his orifices stopped, and no metal vessel or any other cooling object may be placed upon his belly, until the moment he dies.*
>
> *He may not be stirred nor may he be washed, and he should not be laid upon sand or salt, until the moment he dies.*
>
> *His eyes may not be closed. Whosoever touches him or stirs him, sheds blood.*
>
> *Rabbi Meir used to compare a dying man to a flickering lamp; the moment one touches it, he puts it out. So, too, whosoever closes the eyes of a dying man is accounted as though he had snuffed out the man's life. (Semachot 1:1-4)*

The obvious reason behind these laws is that it is forbidden to hasten death in even the slightest way. This poses two questions:

1. **What positive measures must be taken to preserve life?**

2. **Are there any circumstances where the preservation of life is not mandatory, i.e., is euthanasia permitted?**

    Euthanasia (mercy killing) means putting someone to death painlessly in order to avoid prolonged pain of an incurable disease. Is prolonging life artificially, where there is no hope of recovery - thereby adding pain, expense, and intolerable burden to the patient and his family - required? We shall discuss this in greater detail below.

THE ART OF HEALING[21]

The Rabbis had an affirmative attitude toward the art of healing. Today, when medicine has such a prominent role in our civilization and in our daily life for very practical reasons, it is hard to realize that there could be any objection to it. To us, promoting health - largely through medicine - is a most natural and human desire. However, there are certain sects even today that object to medical treatment of illness because of religious scruples, and which, as a matter of principle, would forbid the physician to practice his profession.

---

[21] Adapted from A Time to Be Born A Time to Die, By Rabbi Isaac Klein, United Synagogue Youth, 1988.

In Jewish tradition healing the sick was both a privilege and an obligation. The Rabbis therefore emphasized that not only is the physician permitted to heal, but is actually obligated to do so as a *Mitzvah*, a religious commandment. In their usual way, they derived this principle from an interpretation of a verse of the Bible. The passage that deals with the bodily damage done by one person to another - assault and *Battery* - prescribes:

אִם־יָקוּם וְהִתְהַלֵּךְ בַּחוּץ עַל־מִשְׁעַנְתּוֹ וְנִקָּה הַמַּכֶּה
רַק שִׁבְתּוֹ יִתֵּן וְרַפֹּא יְרַפֵּא:

If he rises again, and walks out with his staff, then shall he who struck him be acquitted; only he shall pay for the loss of his time, and shall cause him to be thoroughly healed.
(Shmot 21:19)

The English word "thoroughly" is an effort to convey the meaning of the repetition in the original Hebrew of the words "he shall heal." To the Rabbis the repetition implied, *"Hence we infer that permission has been granted to the physician to heal (Sandhedrin 61a)."* The Codes - the books of Jewish Law which serve as guides to our religious practice - are even more emphatic, and make healing obligatory. Thus we are told, *"The Torah gave permission to the physician to heal. It is a religious commandment and is included, indeed, in the obligation to save life .... If the physician refrains from healing, he is guilty of shedding blood (Yoreh Deah 361:1)."*

Clearly Judaism places a strong emphasis on preserving life, but does it forbid us from easing the pain of those who are suffering?

EUTHANASIA

Now the opposite question presents itself. Is the preservation of life absolute and unconditional, or are there times when one is not obligated to preserve and prolong life, but is even advised to help terminate it? We are touching here on the question of euthanasia, or "mercy killing." This is not a new problem; there have been euthanasia societies in past generations. It has now reappeared most forcefully because advances in medicine which enable doctors to prolong life by artificial means have given the problem a new dimension.

In the 1990's, in a very public way, Dr. Jack Kevorkian helped scores of terminally ill people who wished to end their lives, to do so. The actions of Dr. Kevorkian have made it a topic of discussion in many homes. An incident related in the Talmud sheds light on the traditional Jewish attitude toward this question. The Talmud tells that Rabbi Judah the Prince fell ill. Everyone prayed for his recovery. Then, "Rabbi's [Rabbi Judah's] handmaid went up on the roof and prayed, `The immortals desire Rabbi, and the mortals desire Rabbi; may it be the will of God that the mortals overpower the immortals.' When, however, she saw how often he resorted to the *Bat*hroom, painfully taking off his phylacteries and putting them on again, she prayed, 'May it be the will of the Almighty that the immortals overpower the mortals.' As the Rabbis incessantly continued their prayer for heavenly mercy, she took up a jar and threw it down from the roof to the ground. For a moment they ceased praying, and the soul of Rabbi departed to its eternal rest (*Ketubot* 104a)."

The analogy and its implications for us should be obvious. When the prolongation of life is merely the prolongation of pain, it is preferable to let nature take its course. In order to spell out the implications, there are several questions we must clarify first.

1. **The obligation of the physician to preserve life for as long as possible is based on the principle that life is good. As such, do we have the right to set limitations and make distinctions, such as between active euthanasia, where the physician administers a drug that will hasten death in terminal cases, and passive**

euthanasia, where the physician refrains from using artificial means to keep the patient alive and merely lets nature take its course?

2. If we should make such distinctions and exceptions, do we not open the door to abuse? The most flagrant example of such abuse was the Nazis' policy of compulsory euthanasia, inaugurated by Hitler's order on September 1, 1939, in which 275,000 people perished in German euthanasia centers. To be sure, this was an extreme case, perpetrated by a monster, the like of which appears once in a millennium. Nevertheless, it makes us conscious of the ever-present fear that exists whenever a third person has to decide on the application of euthanasia, whether that person is acting out of compassion, greed, or some other motive.

3. What about a case where medicine used for alLeviating the patient's pain also shortens his life? May such analgesics (pain relievers) be applied, or must we desist, since using them would make us guilty of shortening a life, which is obviously forbidden?

4. So far we have spoken of persons other than the patient making such decisions, since in most of these cases the patient himself is not able to make a decision or even give an opinion. Should it not be incumbent upon us to develop some way of finding out his opinion, when this is still possible?

To these questions, we have the following answers. There is indeed a difference of opinion among rabbinic authorities about whether to permit euthanasia at all, because of the danger of abuse we mentioned. The majority opinion, however, maintains that with the proper safeguards, we should permit what is termed passive euthanasia. We are not obligated to prolong life artificially where there is no chance of recovery. Thus, the Shulhan Aruch says,

> *"If, however, there is something that causes a delay in the exit of the soul, as for example if near to this house there is a sound of pounding as one who is chopping wood, or there is salt on his tongue and these delay the soul's leaving the body, it is permitted to remove these, because there is no direct act involved here, only the removal of an obstacle." (Yoreh De'ah 339:1)*

The following statements of Rabbi Yehudah Hehassid (d.1217) are even more explicit:

> *"One may not cause the slowing of the dying process. For example, if one was dying [goses] and another person near to that house was chopping wood and because of this the soul was not able to depart, they remove the wood chopper from there." (Margulies, Sefer Hasidim, par. 723)*

The following is even clearer:

> *"One should not cry out upon him (today we would say, `apply artificial stimulants') that his soul should return since he cannot live thereby but a short time (lit. a few days) and those days he will suffer pain (Margulies, Sefer Hasidim, par. 234)."*

There is now the practice of writing a "living will," in which a person asks that his life not be prolonged artificially when there is no hope for recovery.

The Committee on Jewish Law and Standards has grappled repeatedly with this issue. In a response issued in 1998, the Committee ruled that, "A Jew may not commit suicide, ask others to help in committing suicide, or assist in the suicide of someone else. Withholding or withdrawing machines or medications from a terminally ill patient, however, does not constitute suicide and is permitted... one may also withhold or withdraw artificial nutrition and hydration from such a patient, for that too falls outside the prohibitions of suicide and assisted suicide."

Two Rabbis Look at End-of-Life Issues

Rabbi Avram Israel Reisner, "A Halakhic Ethic of Care for the Terminally Ill" YD 339:1.1990a

That which is of the body, of natural function, should be allowed to function. Thus, the withholding or withdrawing of medication, nutrition or hydration is prohibited, so long as they are believed to be beneficial for the prolongation of life. That which is not of the body, but rather which mechanically reproduces, supersedes or circumvents the body's functions (for example, respirators, mechanical pumps, blood purifiers), may be removed as an impediment to death.

Feeding tubes may not be removed from those in permanent vegetative states, as they are not terminally ill.

The patient has autonomy to choose between treatment options in a situation where risk and uncertain prognosis exist. If, however, a particular treatment guarantees a cure, it may not be refused. The only choice which is *barr*ed is the choice to die.

Terminally ill patients may choose hospice or home care.

A patient may reject CPR and/or issue a DNR order when these measures are unlikely to restore the patient to meaningfully healthy life.

Pain treatment should be pursued, but pain medication must be capped at the point at which its probable effect would be to hasten the patient's death.

Rabbi Elliot N. Dorff, "A Jewish Approach to End-Stage Medical Care" YD 339:1.1990b

The key category for dealing with end-of-life issues is *terefah*.

When the patient has an irreversible, terminal illness, medications and other forms of therapy may be withheld or withdrawn. Artificial nutrition and hydration may be considered a sub-category of medication in such circumstances, and therefore may also be withheld or withdrawn.

The category of *terefah* may also be applied to the person in a permanent vegetative state, and it would be permissible to remove artificial nutrition and hydration.

Terminally ill persons may, if they choose, engage in any medical regimen which has the slightest chance of reversing their prognosis so long as the intention is to find a cure, they may do so even if they thereby simultaneously increase the risk of hastening death.

Jewish law includes permission for the patient to refuse any treatment he/she cannot bear, including forms of therapy which, though life-sustaining, the patient judges not to be for his/her benefit.

Terminally ill patients may chose hospice or home care.

A patient may reject CPR and/or issue a DNR order when these measures are unlikely to restore the patient to meaningfully healthy life.

Pain medication may continue even if its probable effect is to hasten the patient's death.

In the spirit of the talmudic interrogative *Mai beinaihu?* [22] The subcommittee on Biomedical Ethics of the CJLS undertook a careful consideration of the practical differences of law that remain between the presentations of Rabbi Reisner and Rabbi Dorff. It was felt that, although the

---

[22] Used with permission from the Rabbinical Assembly.

legal reasoning differs strongly, both papers tend toward a consensus of treatment in most areas, which would perhaps obviate the need to fight it out on theoretical grounds. The following are our conclusions:

The primary difference in theory between the positions of Rabbi Reisner and Rabbi Dorff may be summarized by their key phrases: in Rabbi Reisner's words, "Neither the quality of the life nor its likely short duration is admitted as a mitigating circumstance," as against Rabbi Dorff, "The fetus and the *tereifah* are both cases of human beings whose blood is indeed judged to be 'less red' than that of viable people." Rabbi Reisner insists on the inviolability of the principle of protecting even *hayei sha'ah*, life of short duration, whereas Rabbi Dorff feels that principle is made moot by the status of *tereifah* and the need to consider the patient's best interests (*avdidnan letovato*). Rabbi Dorff might center his objection to Rabbi Reisner's paper in the comment that it is too literalist and not sufficiently alert to the real emotional needs of patients and their families. Rabbi Reisner might frame his objection to Rabbi Dorff's paper in the comment that it arrives at its sensitivity to patients by degrading the status of their God-given lives, which we are constrained not to do.

Nevertheless, both agree in principle and practice on the large area of autonomy that the patient holds with regard to his own treatment where risk and prognostic uncertainty, as they almost always do. Thus, both would allow patients to rule certain treatment options off limits, to choose hospice care as a treatment option, and to draft advance directive documents but only within the parameters established to be in accord with Jewish law. Both permit withdrawal of mechanical life support where unsupported life has been shown to be impossible, under the primary precedent of removing impediments to the death of a *goseis*. Both are in agreement concerning the use of CPR and DNR orders, though for fundamentally different reasons. They agree that CPR need not be done when it is unlikely to succeed in restoring the patient to a meaningfully healthy life. That is perforce a medical judgement call. It is not clear that they would adjudge all cases equally, but on a case-by-case basis, this judgement will fall neither to Rabbi Dorff nor to Rabbi Reisner, but to the family's attending physician, and any member of the clergy advising the family.

The points on which Rabbis Dorff and Reisner differ are few, but significant.

A. With regard to medication to treat a terminally ill patient and with regard to artificial nutrition/hydration:

Rabbi Dorff would permit withholding or withdrawing such medication, since the patient is categorized as a *tereifah*, whose life does not require our full protection. Rabbi Dorff would assimilate artificial nutrition/hydration to medication in such a case.

Rabbi Reisner would prohibit withholding medication, nutrition, or hydration as long as they are believed to be beneficial, since we are obligated to maintain even *hayei sha'ah* (N.B.: and as long as the patient has not ruled out said treatment in a valid treatment directive).

B. With regard to the patient in a persistent vegetative state:

Rabbi Dorff would permit withholding/withdrawal of artificial nutrition and hydration, viewing this patient, like the *tereifah*, as an impared life (N.B.: after due tests and time, of course).

Rabbi Reisner finds no grounds for denying even this limited life, and therefore requires full maintenance pending God's own determination.

C. With regard to pain relief:

Both Rabbis Dorff and Reisner regard treatment for pain as medical treatment to be pursued. They differ on the question of "double effect" -- of whether pain medication must be capped at that point at which its probable effect would be to hasten the patient's death.

Rabbi Dorff argues that the intent to al*Levi*ate pain controls. Rabbi Reisner argues that the probable result controls. Although they do not argue this point clearly in terms of the primary premises of their papers, it appears clear that Rabbi Reisner's concern for *hayei sha'ah* and Rabbi Dorff's vacating of that principle inform their rulings here.

Both Rabbis Dorff and Reisner point out, however, that the best medicine available today should permit sufficient relief of pain without approaching this dilemma; both hope that is quickly recedes to a footnote about antiquated medical ethical problems.

D. A minor note:

Rabbi Dorff's reasoning and a citation of his source, Dr. Sinclair, in chapter 19, appear to permit the early termination of a terminally ill patient for purposes of saving life through organ transplants. It is clear that Rabbi Reisner would disapprove. It is unclear whether Rabbi Dorff would care to proceed, in fact, upon the logic of that position.

We note these matters in this statement of reconciliation so that both powerful attempts to deal with on of today's greatest ethical and halakhic dilemmas might be properly read and understood side by side. We believe that both represent cogent, Conservative responses to the demands of God's Torah and our times, and commend them, as such, to the attention of the full Committee on Jewish Law and Standards.

A summary statement submitted to the Rabbinical Assembly Committee on Jewish Law and Standards, Dec. 1990

death and dying

Note

This section is not meant to be an exhaustive explanation of Jewish mourning practices, but rather an overview of themes that are prevalent in those practices. For more information, refer to the USY source book, *A Time to Be Born, A Time to Die*, by Rabbi Isaac Klein, or *The Jewish Way in Death and Mourning* by Maurice Lamm. Decisions regarding how and when to mourn a relative should be made by the family in consultation with your local rabbi.

A TIME TO DIE

How should someone respond when one hears that...

> **Someone is sick?**

> **Someone was in a bad accident?**

> **Someone has died?**

A rabbi came across an old man who was planting a tree. "Why are you planting a tree?" asked the rabbi. "Do you expect to see it full-grown in your time?" "No," responded the old man, "but the trees I have enjoyed in my lifetime were planted by those before me, so I am planting for those after me."

Why does the man care to plant the trees for future generations?

Why shouldn't he just worry about himself?

None of us is capable of comprehending the end. We strive for immortality because we view death as a mystery, and as a defeat. Nevertheless, the Jewish laws of mourning are widely recognized as the most sensitive, helpful, and psychologically healthy means of dealing with death. Our tradition understands that the initial impact of death upon an individual is one of a gradual process of shock, anger, guilt, and despair. Judaism creates a system of mourning which keeps the mourner from becoming isolated from the community. The Jewish process of grieving, from *Shivah* to *Kaddish*, is designed to help mourners remember their loved ones and be comforted. The laws serve to channel these emotions into a productive expression of grief. In essence, our attitude toward death is shaped by our concept of life. The rites of mourning are for the living, not for the dead.

LOOKING BACK

What did previous generations leave you?

Which things did they leave you intentionally, such as the trees in the story?

What did they leave inadvertently?

What would you like to leave to the next generations?

What sort of world would you like them to have?

Grief is a strong emotion that fills many mourners. Psychologist Elizabeth Kubler-Ross lists 5 Stages of Grief :

Denial – This isn't happening to me!

Anger – Why is this happening to me?

*Bar*gaining – I promise that I'll be a better person if…

Depression – I don't care anymore.

Acceptance – I'm ready for whatever comes.

These stages may begin even before the loved one has passed away, particularly if death is the inevitable outcome of an illness or injury. The Jewish process of mourning is designed to allow a person to pass through these stages in the company of friends and family.

It is especially important to note that while the law provides clear and specific ways of mourning, it also states emphatically that one should not grieve too much. When each period of mourning is over, the mourner should not continue the practices of that stage in the mistaken belief that the more one mourns, the more he displays his love for the deceased. The *Shulhan Aruch* states clearly: *One should not grieve too much for the dead, and whoever grieves excessively is really grieving for someone else (i.e., will probably end up having to mourn for another loss) (Yoreh Deah, Chapter 394:1).*

When a person dies, his close relatives are faced with two tasks:

1. **Making decisions about care of the body and its burial;**

2. **Facing the reality of the death and their own feelings about it.**

Discuss what some of those decisions and emotions might be, and record them below.

Decisions	Emotions

WHO MOURNS?

The law prescribes that only the immediate family mourns. This means: father, mother, brother, sister, son, daughter, husband, and wife. One may mourn for a father-in-law or mother-in-law out of respect for one's spouse. The issues can get very complex. For example, in the case of a divorce, should one mourn for a former spouse? The answer is that this is not necessary, as it may cause problems for the new spouse. By mourning over the former spouse, the mourner may relive the original feelings of love for that person, which—in turn—could create jealousy and hostility by the new spouse. Our tradition always attempts to give priority to the present, rather than the past.

1. **Why does Jewish tradition limit who is required to mourn?**

2. **Given the text from the Shulhan Arukch mentioned in the previous section, do we allow extended family to observe the practices of Jewish mourning?**

3. **What can these extended family members do to honor the deceased?**

Another interesting area of complexity is in the case of a convert to Judaism. What if his parent dies? A recent response issued by the Committee on Jewish Law and Standards dictates that the convert should observe all of the practices of mourning when a non-Jewish relative dies. This enables the convert to take advantage of the structure and comfort offered by Jewish bereavement practices and does not demean his grief.

WHO IS MOURNED OVER?

With certain exceptions and various shades of opinion, the deceased must be over 30 days old before dying, to require mourning over. An infant who dies within its first 30 days of life is simply buried, without any formal mourning practices. We do not mourn over an apostate (one who converts out of Judaism), one who is cremated (although there are differing opinions), a criminal who is executed (assuming he would have been executed under Jewish law, also), and a suicide. (We do often go out of our way to prove extenuating circumstances—such as temporary insanity—existed, taking such a death out of the realm of suicide. This is to avoid humiliation to the family.)

KAVOD HAMET – HONORING THE DEAD

When hearing of death, one says: בָּרוּךְ דַּיַן הָאֱמֶת *"Praised be the righteous Judge."*

How do you feel saying these words upon hearing about the death of someone you knew?

How do you feel saying these words about the death of a close relative?

Why do we speak of God as a judge at time of death?

When else do we refer to God as a judge? (Think about the daily liturgy in the siddur.)

One way of understanding these words is that they acknowledge the fact that there are some things in life over which we human beings have no control. Death is surely one of those things. For those who might feel guilt or responsibility upon hearing of the death of someone they knew, saying these words is recognition that they personally had nothing to do with causing the death. For those who are less intimately involved, the words are a reminder that people do not control the time of death – and are not in control of many things that are central to the human experience.

ORGAN DONATION[23]

The Rabbinical Assembly Committee on Jewish Law and Standards has ruled that one is obligated to permit postmortem transplantation of his or her organs in lifesaving medical procedures and that withholding consent for such organ donation in contrary to Jewish Law.

ORGAN AND TISSUE DONATION INFORMATION[24]

The inestimable value of human life is a cardinal principle of Jewish Law. This value is expressed through the religious obligation for self-preservation, as well as the duty to save the life of one's fellow human being, if he or she is in mortal danger. This religious obligation is a mitzvah of such a high order that it takes precedence over virtually all other religious duties with which it may conflict: the sick must eat on Yom Kippur; the injured are treated on the Sabbath, we postpone the circumcision of weakened infants beyond the covenantally mandated eighth day, etc.

Since the onset of the modern era of organ transplantation in the 1950's, leading rabbinic authorities from throughout the religious spectrum have seen in this new technology a new and effective means of fulfilling a divine mandate to save life—an obligation first expressed in the Torah itself:

---

[23] Reprinted with permission from the Rabbinical Assembly. "Organ and Tissue Donation Card" by Rabbi Joseph H. Prouser. Adopted by the CJLS on June 12, 1996. Pages 191-193, 1991-2000 Responsa.

[24] A Project of the Rabbinical Assembly and the United Synagogue of Conservative Judaism. Developed by the Committee on Jewish Law and Standards of the Rabbinical Assembly.

לֹא־תֵלֵךְ רָכִיל בְּעַמֶּיךָ לֹא תַעֲמֹד עַל־דַּם רֵעֶךָ אֲנִי יְהוָה׃

You shall not stand idly by the blood of your neighbor. (Vayikra 19:16)

Organ donation is a new means to fulfill an ancient, eternal religious duty: a mitzvah of the highest order.

The Committee on Jewish Law and Standards has affirmed this principle in unambiguous terms… Rabbi Joseph H. Prouser[25] who authored the Committee's paper on Organ Donation said, "The preservation of human life is obligatory, not optional. Since all conflicting halakhic duties are suspended and human lives are at stake…consent must be granted for postmortem organ donation when requested by doctors or hospitals for use in lifesaving transplantation procedures. …This applies to the individual in anticipation of his or her own death, as well as to health care proxies or next of kin whenever they are legally empowered to make such decisions on behalf of the deceased….By doing so, he or she renders only profound and genuine honor to the deceased."

Anyone who is able to save a life but fails to do so violates this mitzvah. (Maimonides)

Rabbi David Golinkin, Law Committee Chairman of the Rabbinical Assembly of Israel and Dean of the Seminary of Jewish Studies in Jerusalem felt so strongly he commented that we are actually commanded to donate our organs, "It is not merely permissible for a Jew to bequeath his organs for transplantation following his death, it is a *Mitzvah* for him to do so, in order to save one life, or several lives."

"The overriding principles of honoring the dead (*k'vod ha-met*) and saving lives (*pikuah nefesh*) work in tandem," wrote Rabbi Elliot N. Dorff, Rector, University of Jerusalem. "That is, saving a person's life is so sacred a value in Judaism that if a person's organ can be used to save someone else's life, it is actually an honor to the deceased."

The Need

- Over 68,000 people are waiting for organ transplants

- Of this number, over 2,100 are children

- Many thousands more need donated tissues

- Every 16 minutes a new name is added to the list.

- Typically, 13 patients each day (5,000 each year) die while waiting for their life-saving organ transplant.

The Success

- Most organ transplants are very successful, either saving lives or greatly improving the quality of life for the recipients.

- One-year success rates range from 70% for livers and lungs, to over 90% for kidneys.

- Many of these recipients have had functioning transplants for over 25 years.

---

[25] "The Obligation to Preserve Life and The Question of Post-Mortem Organ Donation," Response adopted by the RA Committee on Jewish Law and Standards)

- Success rates continually improve as better methods to control rejection are identified.
- Typically, 13 patients each day (5,000 each year) die while waiting for their life-saving organ transplant.

The Process

- Collect information about donation and transplantation
- Familiarize yourself with the Jewish obligation to preserve life.
- Talk to your family about your decision
- Sign the donor card at the back of this book in the presence of two witnesses
- Carry the signed card in your purse or wallet with your identification. Include your donor status in any more comprehensive advance medical directives.

Other Information to Help You Decide

- The body of an organ and/or tissue donor is always treated with care and respect.
- There is no charge to the donor or to his or her family for donation.
- Organ and tissue donation will not delay funeral arrangements.
- Studies show that organ donation helps to shorten the time needed by members of a bereaved family to recover from their loss.
- The traditional Jewish belief in resurrection in no way precludes organ donation.

HEVRA KADDISHA

Judaism places great importance on caring for the body of the deceased between death and burial. While many people would find this to be very creepy, this *mitzvah*, *Halvayat HaMet* (accompanying the dead), is often referred to as *Hesed Shel Emet* (the most truthful kindness).

Read the following text from *Bereshit* 47:29 and Rashi's commentary that follows it:

וַיִּקְרְבוּ יְמֵי־יִשְׂרָאֵל לָמוּת וַיִּקְרָא | לִבְנוֹ לְיוֹסֵף וַיֹּאמֶר לוֹ אִם־נָא
מָצָאתִי חֵן בְּעֵינֶיךָ שִׂים־נָא יָדְךָ תַּחַת יְרֵכִי וְעָשִׂיתָ עִמָּדִי חֶסֶד וֶאֱמֶת
אַל־נָא תִקְבְּרֵנִי בְּמִצְרָיִם:

And when the time approached for Israel to die, he summoned his son Joseph and said to him, "Do me this favor, place your hand under my thigh as a pledge of your steadfast loyalty: please do not bury me in Egypt.

חֶסֶד וֶאֱמֶת. חֶסֶד שֶׁעוֹשִׂין עִם הַמֵּתִים הוּא חֶסֶד שֶׁל אֱמֶת' שֶׁאֵינוֹ מְצַפֶּה וְלַתַשְׁלוּם גְּמוּל:

"A true act of kindness" – kindness that is done for the dead is a true act of kindness since one does it without expecting any repayment. (Rashi on Bereshit 47:29)

1. **Why did Israel (Jacob) ask Joseph to do a "true act of kindness?"**

2. **Does Judaism attribute a sense of sanctity to death?**

3. **Why is burying the dead the highest form of lovingkindness – hesed shel emet?**

While the body of the deceased no longer holds life within it, it is still treated with the utmost respect. Religious law, rather than personal sentiment and whim, dictates how the body is cared for following death. The task of preparing the body for burial falls upon the Chevra Kaddisha (burial society) which exists in most major cities.

At no point is the body left alone during this process. A person called a *shomer* (guard or watcher) stays at the body's side at all times. This may be a member of the Chevra Kaddisha, a family member, or a close friend. This person remains awake during the entire period of watching and reads from the Book of Psalms or another appropriate text. While in the room of the deceased, the focus is on the deceased and the funeral arrangements, rather than any personal needs of the people in the room.

It is so important within Judaism to respect the deceased that the rabbis related the following story in the Talmud:

ואמר רב יהודה אמר רב: מת בעיר – כל בני העיר
אסורין בעשיית מלאכה. רב המנונא איקלע לדרומתא' שמע קול שיפורא
דשכבא. חזא הנך אינשי דקא עבדי עבידתא' אמר להו: ליהוו הנך אנשי
בשמתא! לא שכבא איכא במתא? אמרו ליה: חבורתא איכא במתא. – אמר
להו: אי הכי – שריא לכו.

Rav Judah also said this, quoting Rav: "When a person dies in town, all the townspeople are forbidden from doing work." R. Hamnuna once came to Darumata. He heard the sound of the funerary-bugle and seeing some people carrying on their work, he said, "Let the people be under the ban. Is there not a person dead in town?" They told him that there was a Society [to care for the dead] in the town. "If so," he said to them, "you are allowed [to work]." (Mo'ed Katan 27b)

If there had not been a burial society in place to care for the deceased, the entire town would have been forced to stop working and ensure that a proper burial take place.

The preparation consists of three stages:

1. *Taharah* (purification) – This is the washing or purification of the body prior to burial. This act is usually performed by the Chevra Kaddisha. The body is washed thoroughly from head to foot. As in many areas of Jewish purity customs, although hygienic considerations are apparent, it is the spiritual context of purification that is primary. Originally, the custom was for each cemetery to have a *taharah* room for this purpose; today, when almost all funerals take place at funeral parlors, it is done on those premises.

   One may will his eyes, other organs, or tissue of his body for transplantation into other bodies or healing purposes, because there is no greater K'vod HaMet (honor given to the dead) than to bring healing to the living. However, the dead body must be treated respectfully and the remains must be given proper burial.

2. *Tachrichin* (shrouds)--the body is then wrapped in plain white robes, called shrouds. Tradition objects to dressing the deceased in fine clothing. Hence it prescribes the use of shrouds. This was required in order not to em*bar*rass the poor, and also because death is not the time to show one's wealth. The rule goes back to the time of Rabban Gamliel (1st Century C.E.), who noticed that the rich were buried in ostentatious clothes which proved to be an em*bar*rassment to the poor, who could not afford them. He therefore insisted that he be buried in plain shrouds.

3. *Aron* (Coffin) —This must be a plain wooden box - generally with wooden pegs, rather than with nails. This is done to maintain the equality of all in death and to follow the principle of "dust you are and to dust you shall return" (*Bereishit* 3:19). This is also the reason that Judaism does not permit cremation. Some synagogues place *Shaymot* (literally names, but refers to texts containing the name of God) that can no longer be used into the grave.[26]

Jewish tradition frowns upon viewing the body. It has become the prevalent secular custom to have the body on exhibition the night before the funeral. It is part of Jewish practice to keep the coffin closed, out of our desire to have the family remember the deceased as he was in life, not in death. By viewing the corpse, as others do, the image of the dead face will remain in the minds of the viewers forever. We prefer to recall the happy and lively moments that we shared together with our loved one. Jewish tradition has us pay our respects to the deceased at the funeral. Consoling the mourners should begin after the burial, at the home of the mourner. It is also an added burden on the family to be taxed with these social formalities when their hearts are heavy with sorrow, and when they would prefer to be left alone.

KERIYAH

The custom of tearing one's garment upon the death of a relative is called *keriah*. Originally, this was done immediately upon hearing news of the death. For example,

וַיַּחֲזֵק דָּוִד בִּבְגָדָו [בִּבְגָדָיו] וַיִּקְרָעֵם וְגַם כָּל־הָאֲנָשִׁים אֲשֶׁר אִתּוֹ:

David took hold of his clothes and rent them, and so did all the men with him. (II Samuel 1:11)

David takes this action upon hearing of the death of King Saul and his son. Nowadays, it is usually done at the chapel or after the funeral. Custom dictates that the garment is torn on the left side when mourning over a parent and on the right side for any other family member. When keriah is performed, mourners recite the following blessing:

בָּרוּךְ אַתָּה יְיָ אֱלֹהֵינוּ מֶלֶךְ הָעוֹלָם, דַּיַּן הָאֱמֶת

Blessed are you, Lord our God, Ruler of the Universe, who is the Judge of truth.

---

[26] Embalming (treatment of the dead body with drugs or chemicals to prevent decay) is permitted only as a result of specific conditions, such as sanitary reasons, civil law requirements, or the necessary delay of burial. In such cases, embalming is permitted as an act of *K'vod HaMet*. If the embalming process involves the removal of certain parts of the body, those parts should be put into a container and buried together with the body.

Many families choose to utilize a special ribbon (usually provided by the funeral director) that is attached to their clothes and is ripped for them. Some people feel this defeats the purpose of *keriah*, which is to give expression to one's grief, showing a lack of concern with one's clothes. They feel that a ribbon displays the opposite—that the mourner cares more about his clothes than about the loss of a loved one. However, others feel that *keriah* is a symbolic act, anyway, and therefore the ribbon symbolically expresses the same idea that *keriah* on one's clothing does.

Why do you think the ripping of clothing became symbolic of mourning?

Do you feel that ripping a ribbon has the same meaning?

ANINUT

There are basically two stages of mourning: before the burial and after. The period between death and burial is referred to as *aninut*. During this time, the mourner (called an *onen*, at this stage) is exempt from fulfilling any of the *mitzvot*, including wearing *tefillin* and reciting the *Shema*. Rabbi Joseph Soloveitchik[27] explains why:

> Beaten by the friend, his prayers rejected, enveloped by a hideous darkness, forsaken and lonely, man begins to question his own human singular reality. Doubt develops quickly into a cruel conviction, and doubting man turns into mocking man. At whom does man mock? At himself... If death is the final destiny of all men ... then why be a man at all?... why carry the human-moral load? Are we not ... just a band of conceited and inflated daydreamers who somehow manage to convince ourselves of some imaginary superiority over the brutes in the jungle?

Our tradition recognizes this condition, and, therefore, dictates to the mourner that he is not to observe many of the normally required commandments. Rather, he or she should expend all of his or her energy on making the arrangements for the burial, thus following the dictate "He who is occupied with the performance of a *mitzvah* is exempt from the performance of another *mitzvah*" (Babylonian Talmud, Tractate *Sotah* 44b). This is an incredible fact of Jewish life! Our system of laws, statutes and customs, which seems so rigid to outsiders, is so flexible as to allow its absolute disuse. It is the tremendous wisdom inherent in our law that it is deemed inappropriate to expect an individual to remain faithful and loyal to our commands at the very moment that he or she questions his or her own existence as a human, as well as the existence of God, which undoubtedly occurs to a mourner during the first moments of distress.

Therefore, the best advice is formulated by the Rabbi Shimon ben Elazar of the Mishna, who said:

רַבִּי שִׁמְעוֹן בֶּן אֶלְעָזָר אוֹמֵר, אַל תְּרַצֶּה אֶת חֲבֵרְךָ בִּשְׁעַת כַּעֲסוֹ

Do not comfort him when his dead lies before him. (Pirkei Avot 4:23)

---

[27] J. Soloveitchik in "The Halacha of the First Day," in Jack Riemer's <u>Jewish Reflections on Death,</u> 1975 pp. 76-77.

This advice showed great compassion for the perplexed, suffering person, firmly held in the clutches of what he sees as his arch-enemy, death. When man is apt to ask himself, "If everything human terminates, and death is the final destiny of man, why be man at all, why be committed, why carry the human-moral load?" we leave him to his dark thoughts and exempt him from religious commandments that point in the opposite direction. Otherwise, we risk making a hypocrite out of the *onen*.

FUNERAL SERVICE AND BURIAL

There is no standard or fixed funeral service. All complete prayer books and rabbinic manuals have a general form. The service has two parts, one originally recited at home and one at the cemetery. Today, however, the first part is almost always conducted at a funeral parlor rather than at home. The service consists of a Psalm, a scriptural passage, and the Memorial prayer (אֵל מָלֵא רַחֲמִים —*Ayl Maley Rahamim*). The eulogy is now customarily given before the Memorial prayer.

The Talmud wisely declares, "Just as the dead shall be called to account, so shall the eulogizers be called to account," (*Bracho*t 62a) implying that just as it is wrong to overpraise in a eulogy, so it is wrong not to eulogize a deserving person properly.

Originally, eulogies were reserved for persons of distinction, but in the democratic climate of America, eulogies are delivered at all funerals. To be sure, it is forbidden to exaggerate and to attribute virtues to one who never had them, yet it is permitted to be charitable in one's praises. Furthermore, the eulogy may also serve as an opportunity to moralize and dwell on the meaning of life that the living might take it to heart.

If the deceased was a spiritual or community leader, it is the practice in some communities to bring the body into the synagogue and hold the funeral services there.

There is a difference of opinion about the order of the procession when the coffin is carried out of the house or funeral parlor. In some places, the practice is for the mourners to leave first, followed by the coffin (carried by pall bearers) and then the rest of the people. In other places, the coffin is carried out first. Today many have adopted the practice of having the family leave first, followed by the rest of the people, and finally the coffin, carried out by the pall bearers. This practice is simply a matter of convenience, since it gives those attending the opportunity to get into their cars and take their places in the procession. Perhaps this, too, is *K'vod Hamet*, since it spares the hearse with the body the necessity of waiting.

The custom used to be for the pallbearers to carry the coffin on their shoulders to the cemetery, especially if the deceased was a person of distinction. Today, when cemeteries are far from residential areas, the hearse brings the coffin to the cemetery gates; from there it is carried on a platform (called a catafalque) to the grave. Seven stops are usually made. Between the stops, Psalm 91 is recited because of the words of comfort it contains.

א יֹשֵׁב בְּסֵתֶר עֶלְיוֹן בְּצֵל שַׁדַּי יִתְלוֹנָן: ב אֹמַר לַיהוָה מַחְסִי וּמְצוּדָתִי אֱלֹהַי
אֶבְטַח־בּוֹ: ג כִּי הוּא יַצִּילְךָ מִפַּח יָקוּשׁ מִדֶּבֶר הַוּוֹת: ד בְּאֶבְרָתוֹ | יָסֶךְ לָךְ
וְתַחַת כְּנָפָיו תֶּחְסֶה צִנָּה וְסֹחֵרָה אֲמִתּוֹ: ה לֹא־תִירָא מִפַּחַד לָיְלָה מֵחֵץ
יָעוּף יוֹמָם: ו מִדֶּבֶר בָּאֹפֶל יַהֲלֹךְ מִקֶּטֶב יָשׁוּד צָהֳרָיִם: ז יִפֹּל מִצִּדְּךָ | אֶלֶף
וּרְבָבָה מִימִינֶךָ אֵלֶיךָ לֹא יִגָּשׁ: ח רַק בְּעֵינֶיךָ תַבִּיט וְשִׁלֻּמַת רְשָׁעִים תִּרְאֶה:
ט כִּי־אַתָּה יְהוָה מַחְסִי עֶלְיוֹן שַׂמְתָּ מְעוֹנֶךָ: י לֹא־תְאֻנֶּה אֵלֶיךָ רָעָה וְנֶגַע
לֹא־יִקְרַב בְּאָהֳלֶךָ: יא כִּי מַלְאָכָיו יְצַוֶּה־לָּךְ לִשְׁמָרְךָ בְּכָל־דְּרָכֶיךָ:

יב עַל־כַּפַּיִם יִשָּׂאוּנְךָ פֶּן־תִּגֹּף בָּאֶבֶן רַגְלֶךָ: יג עַל־שַׁחַל וָפֶתֶן תִּדְרֹךְ תִּרְמֹס
כְּפִיר וְתַנִּין: יד כִּי בִי חָשַׁק וַאֲפַלְּטֵהוּ אֲשַׂגְּבֵהוּ כִּי־יָדַע שְׁמִי: טו יִקְרָאֵנִי |
וְאֶעֱנֵהוּ עִמּוֹ אָנֹכִי בְצָרָה אֲחַלְּצֵהוּ וַאֲכַבְּדֵהוּ: טז אֹרֶךְ יָמִים אַשְׂבִּיעֵהוּ
וְאַרְאֵהוּ בִּישׁוּעָתִי:

1. He who dwells in the secret place of the most High, who abides under the shadow of the Almighty, 2. Will say to the Lord, My refuge and my fortress, my God, in whom I trust, 3. For He shall save you from the snare of the fowler, and from the noisome pestilence. 4. He shall cover you with His feathers, and under His wings shall you find refuge; His truth shall be your shield and buckler. 5. You shall not be afraid of the terror by night; nor of the arrow that flies by day; 6. Nor of the pestilence that walks in darkness; nor of the destruction that wastes at noonday. 7. A thousand shall fall at your side, and ten thousand at your right hand; but it shall not come near you. 8. Only with your eyes shall you behold and see the reward of the wicked. 9. Because you, O Lord, are my refuge. You have made the most High your habitation; 10. No evil shall befall you, nor shall any plague come near your dwelling.11. For He shall give His angels charge over you, to keep you in all your ways. 12. They shall carry you up in their hands, lest you dash your foot against a stone. 13. You shall tread on the lion and on the adder; the young lion and the crocodile shall you trample under foot. 14. Because he has set his love upon me, therefore I will save him; I will set him on high, because he knows My name. 15. He shall call upon Me, and I will answer him; I will be with him in trouble; I will save him, and honor him. 16. With long life I will satisfy him, and show him my salvation.

After the coffin has been placed in the grave, several spadefuls of earth were traditionally put over it before the start of the service. Naturally, the burial service has a tremendous impact on the mourners, and the sound of dirt landing on the coffin can be a very sobering reminder of death's reality. In some communities, the coffin is covered with a carpet simulating grass. Others simply lower the coffin and cover it with earth after the service.

The service at the grave begins with *Tzidduk Hadin*, which is a justification of divine judgment (the essential idea of the burial service), and with a prayer for the survivors. The *Tzidduk Hadin* is rich with biblical verses, expressing our sense of resignation and our continuing faith in God, despite the pain and the loss we feel.

The Rock, His work is perfect and all His ways are just; a faithful God, never false, true and upright is He. The Rock is perfect in every way. Who can question Him about His deeds? God rules below and on high, causing death and giving life to the dead, bringing down to the grave and raising up…. Adonai has given and Adonai has taken; praise by the name of Adonai. God, being merciful, grants atonement for sin and does not destroy. Time and again God restrains wrath and refuses to let rage be all consuming.[28]

On days when *Tahanun* (penitential supplication) is not said in the daily service, *Tzidduk Hadin* is omitted, and Psalm 16, expressing similar sentiments, is recited instead.

א מִכְתָּם לְדָוִד שָׁמְרֵנִי אֵל כִּי־חָסִיתִי בָךְ: ב אָמַרְתְּ לַיהוָה אֲדֹנָי אָתָּה טוֹבָתִי
בַּל־עָלֶיךָ: ג לִקְדוֹשִׁים אֲשֶׁר־בָּאָרֶץ הֵמָּה וְאַדִּירֵי כָּל־חֶפְצִי־בָם: ד יִרְבּוּ עַצְּבוֹתָם
אַחֵר מָהָרוּ בַּל־אַסִּיךְ נִסְכֵּיהֶם מִדָּם וּבַל־אֶשָּׂא אֶת־שְׁמוֹתָם עַל־שְׂפָתָי: ה יְהוָה
מְנָת־חֶלְקִי וְכוֹסִי אַתָּה תּוֹמִיךְ גּוֹרָלִי: ו חֲבָלִים נָפְלוּ־לִי בַּנְּעִמִים אַף־נַחֲלָת
שָׁפְרָה עָלָי: ז אֲבָרֵךְ אֶת־יְהוָה אֲשֶׁר יְעָצָנִי אַף־לֵילוֹת יִסְּרוּנִי כִלְיוֹתָי: ח שִׁוִּיתִי

[28] Translation excerpted from The Rabbinical Assembly Rabbi's Manual, E-60. Several paragraphs omitted.

יְהֹוָה לְנֶגְדִּי תָמִיד כִּי מִימִינִי בַּל־אֶמּוֹט: ט לָכֵן | שָׂמַח לִבִּי וַיָּגֶל כְּבוֹדִי אַף־בְּשָׂרִי יִשְׁכֹּן לָבֶטַח: י כִּי | לֹא־תַעֲזֹב נַפְשִׁי לִשְׁאוֹל לֹא־תִתֵּן חֲסִידְךָ לִרְאוֹת שָׁחַת: יא תּוֹדִיעֵנִי אֹרַח חַיִּים שֹׂבַע שְׂמָחוֹת אֶת־פָּנֶיךָ נְעִמוֹת בִּימִינְךָ נֶצַח:

1. A Miktam of David. Preserve me, O God; for in You I put my trust. 2. I have said to the Lord, You are my Lord; I have no good apart from You; 3. As for the holy ones who are in the earth, they are the excellent, in whom is all my delight. 4. And for those who choose another god, their sorrows shall be multiplied; their drink offerings of blood I will not offer, nor take up their names upon my lips. 5. The Lord is the portion of my inheritance and of my cup; You maintain my lot. 6. The lines are fallen for me in pleasant places; I have a goodly heritage. 7. I will bless the Lord, who has given me counsel; my insides also instruct me in the night seasons. 8. I have set the Lord always before me; because He is at my right hand, I shall not be moved. 9. Therefore my heart is glad, and my glory rejoices; my flesh also dwells secure. 10. For You will not abandon my soul to Sheol; nor will You suffer your pious one to see the pit. 11.You will show me the path of life; in Your presence is fullness of joy; at Your right hand there are pleasures for evermore.

This is followed by the Memorial prayer, *Ayl Maley Rahamim*, a prayer for the peace of the departed soul.

In memory of a male

אֵל מָלֵא רַחֲמִים שׁוֹכֵן בַּמְּרוֹמִים. הַמְצֵא מְנוּחָה נְכוֹנָה תַּחַת כַּנְפֵי הַשְּׁכִינָה. בְּמַעֲלוֹת קְדוֹשִׁים וּטְהוֹרִים כְּזֹהַר הָרָקִיעַ מַזְהִירִים אֶת נִשְׁמַת בֶּן־ _____ שֶׁהָלַךְ לְעוֹלָמוֹ, בְּגַן עֵדֶן תְּהֵא מְנוּחָתוֹ. אָנָּא, בַּעַל הָרַחֲמִים הַסְתִּירֵהוּ בְּסֵתֶר כְּנָפֶיךָ לְעוֹלָמִים. וּצְרוֹר בִּצְרוֹר הַחַיִּים אֶת נִשְׁמָתוֹ. יְיָ הוּא נַחֲלָתוֹ: וְיָנוּחַ בְּשָׁלוֹם עַל מִשְׁכָּבוֹ. וְנֹאמַר אָמֵן:

In memory of a female

אֵל מָלֵא רַחֲמִים שׁוֹכֵן בַּמְּרוֹמִים. הַמְצֵא מְנוּחָה נְכוֹנָה תַּחַת כַּנְפֵי הַשְּׁכִינָה. בְּמַעֲלוֹת קְדוֹשִׁים וּטְהוֹרִים כְּזֹהַר הָרָקִיעַ מַזְהִירִים אֶת נִשְׁמַת בַּת־ _____ שֶׁהָלְכָה לְעוֹלָמָהּ, בְּגַן עֵדֶן תְּהֵא מְנוּחָתָהּ. אָנָּא, בַּעַל הָרַחֲמִים הַסְתִּירֶהָ בְּסֵתֶר כְּנָפֶיךָ לְעוֹלָמִים. וּצְרוֹר בִּצְרוֹר הַחַיִּים אֶת נִשְׁמָתָהּ. יְיָ הוּא נַחֲלָתָהּ: וְתָנוּחַ בְּשָׁלוֹם עַל מִשְׁכָּבָהּ. וְנֹאמַר אָמֵן:

For both males and females:

אֵל מָלֵא רַחֲמִים-- *Exalted, compassionate God, grant infinite rest, in Your sheltering Presence, among the holy and pure, to the soul of _____, who has gone to (his/her) eternal home. Merciful One, we ask that our loved one find perfect peace in Your eternal embrace. May (hi/her) soul be bound up in the bond of life. May (he/she) rest in peace. And let us say: Amen.*

The *Kaddish*, recited by the mourners, closes the service. We will examine the *Kaddish* further below.

After the service the people present form two lines, and the mourners pass between them. As they pass, the people offer their condolences with the traditional

הַמָּקוֹם יְנַחֵם אֶתְכֶם בְּתוֹךְ שְׁאָר אֲבֵלֵי צִיּוֹן וִירוּשָׁלָיִם

"May the Holy One, blessed be He, comfort you among the other mourners for Zion and Jerusalem."

Before leaving the cemetery, those present wash their hands. In some places the practice is to wash the hands before entering the house to which the mourners return.

There is also a custom of plucking some grass when leaving the burial grounds, and saying,

יְהִי פִסַּת־בַּר | בָּאָרֶץ בְּרֹאשׁ הָרִים יִרְעַשׁ כַּלְּבָנוֹן
פִּרְיוֹ וְיָצִיצוּ מֵעִיר כְּעֵשֶׂב הָאָרֶץ:

"And they may blossom out of the city like grass of the earth" (Psalms 72:16)

and

כִּי הוּא יָדַע יִצְרֵנוּ זָכוּר כִּי־עָפָר אֲנָחְנוּ:

"He remembers that we are dust" (Psalms 103:14).

Both are at once emblematic of the frailties of life, and the hope for resurrection and immortality.

KADDISH

A common misperception is that the *Kaddish* is a prayer about death. A version of it is, of course, recited by mourners beginning after burial. The *Kaddish*, however, is actually an affirmation of life, proclaiming the eternity of God, God's mercy, and God's sovereignty. There is no mention of death or the dead in the text. Instead, it is an affirmation of life and faith.

Kaddish comes from the same root as the word *Kadosh* and can be translated as holy. This declaration of God's holiness can only be recited when there is a *minyan* (a quorum of ten Jewish adults). This constitutes the smallest size at which a Jewish community can function.

There are several variations of the *Kaddish*. The longest version of the *Kaddish*, *Kaddish D'rabanan* (the Rabbi's *Kaddish*), is recited after studying rabbinic texts. *Kaddish Shalem* (the Full *Kaddish*) and the *Chatzi Kaddish* (Half *Kaddish*) are recited at various points during services as divisions between different sections of prayer.

Recitation of the *Kaddish* is a way of saying, "Death, be not proud!" It starts the mourner's slow progress in the reassertion of life. Through its recitation, mourners can look towards the future and begin a process of healing.

Reader:

יִתְגַּדַּל וְיִתְקַדַּשׁ שְׁמֵהּ רַבָּא בְּעָלְמָא דִּי־הוּא עָתִיד לְאִתְחַדָּתָא וּלְאַחֲיָאה
מֵתַיָּה וּלְאַסָּקָא יָתְהוֹן לְחַיֵּי עָלְמָא. וּלְמִבְנֵא קַרְתָּא דִּי־יְרוּשְׁלֵם
וּלְשַׁכְלָלָא הֵיכְלֵהּ בְּגַוֵּהּ. וּלְמֶעְקַר פָּלְחָנָא נֻכְרָאָה מִן אַרְעָא וְלַאֲתָבָא
פָּלְחָנָא דִּי־שְׁמַיָּא לְאַתְרֵהּ. וְיַמְלִיךְ קֻדְשָׁא בְּרִיךְ הוּא בְּמַלְכוּתֵהּ וִיקָרֵהּ

בְּחַיֵּיכוֹן וּבְיוֹמֵיכוֹן וּבְחַיֵּי דִּי־כָל־בֵּית יִשְׂרָאֵל. בַּעֲגָלָא וּבִזְמַן קָרִיב וְאִמְרוּ אָמֵן:

Hallowed and enhanced may He be throughout the world of His own creation. May He cause His sovereignty soon to be accepted, during our life and the life of all Israel. And let us say: Amen.

Congregation and Reader:

יְהֵא שְׁמֵהּ רַבָּא מְבָרַךְ לְעָלַם וּלְעָלְמֵי עָלְמַיָּא:

May He be praised throughout all time.

Reader:

יִתְבָּרַךְ וְיִשְׁתַּבַּח וְיִתְפָּאַר וְיִתְרוֹמַם וְיִתְנַשֵּׂא וְיִתְהַדָּר וְיִתְעַלֶּה וְיִתְהַלָּל שְׁמֵהּ דְּקֻדְשָׁא בְּרִיךְ הוּא לְעֵלָּא (בעשי״ת וּלְעֵלָּא מִכָּל) מִן כָּל בִּרְכָתָא וְשִׁירָתָא תֻּשְׁבְּחָתָא וְנֶחֱמָתָא, דַּאֲמִירָן בְּעָלְמָא, וְאִמְרוּ אָמֵן:

Glorified and celebrated, lauded and worshiped, acclaimed and honored, extolled and exalted may the Holy One be, praised beyond all song and psalm, beyond all tributes which mortals can utter. And let us say: Amen.

יְהֵא שְׁלָמָא רַבָּא מִן שְׁמַיָּא, וְחַיִּים (טוֹבִים) עָלֵינוּ וְעַל כָּל יִשְׂרָאֵל וְאִמְרוּ אָמֵן.

Let there be abundant peace from Heaven, with life's goodness for us and for all the people Israel. And let us say: Amen.

עֹשֶׂה שָׁלוֹם בִּמְרוֹמָיו הוּא יַעֲשֶׂה שָׁלוֹם עָלֵינוּ וְעַל כָּל יִשְׂרָאֵל, וְאִמְרוּ אָמֵן:

He who brings peace to His universe will bring peace to us and to all the people Israel. And let us say: Amen.

1. **Why would the rabbis have mourners recite a text about God as part of the mourning process? What was there goal?**

2. **What themes are present in the *Kaddish*?**

The *Kaddish Yatom* (the Mourner's *Kaddish*) differs from the *Kaddish Shalem* (Full *Kaddish*) in only one place. The *Kaddish Yatom* excludes the following line:

תִּתְקַבֵּל צְלוֹתְהוֹן וּבָעוּתְהוֹן דְּכָל (בֵּית) יִשְׂרָאֵל קֳדָם אֲבוּהוֹן דִּי בִשְׁמַיָּא וְאִמְרוּ אָמֵן:

May the prayers and pleas of the whole House of Israel be accepted by our Father in Heaven. And let us say: Amen.

Why would mourners not say a line about having their prayers and pleas answered?

SEUDAT HAVRA'AH

From the will of Rabbi Eliezer the Great, who lived during the 11th century:

My son! Comfort the mourners, and speak to their heart. The companions of Job were held punishable merely because they reproached when they should have consoled him. Thus it is written, "Ye have not spoken of Me the thing that is right, as My servant Job hath."

Jewish tradition involves the whole Jewish community in helping a mourner overcome the shock and sorrow of bereavement. When we help the mourner, we bring out what is best and most human in us.

Avelut, full mourning, begins immediately after the funeral.

Upon returning to the house, a bowl, pitcher of water, and towels are usually placed outside for the mourners and those who accompanied them to the cemetery. This ritual washing reflects the belief that contact with the deceased makes one ritually impure.

On the first day of mourning (which begins immediately after the burial) the family is directed not to prepare its own meals. It is a *mitzvah* for the friends and consolers to prepare their first meal. This is called a *Se'udat Havra'ah* (meal of consolation). The practical reason for this arrangement is that the mourners are not likely to think of preparing food or of eating. Another reason is that the meal and the community support serve as a source of comfort and consolation. The mourners usually suffer from a sense of guilt, a feeling of loneliness, or of being forsaken by man and God. Having friends provide and serve the first meal shows the mourners in a very concrete way that other people do care about them.

At the *Se'udat Havra'ah*, the foods served have a symbolic meaning, and enhance the aspect of comfort and consolation to the mourners. They lessen the feeling of guilt by reminding the mourner that death is the fate of all people. The meal usually contains foods that are round, such as eggs, lentils, chickpeas, etc. – symbolizing the wheel of fate that spares no one as it turns. Eggs have an additional meaning: they are a symbol of new life, hope, and regeneration.

Through some of the laws of mourning, we can see the interaction of Jewish ethical values and law. For the *Seu'dat Hevra'ah*, the food used to be brought to the family in a wicker basket. This is because in ancient times, the rich would bring the food on silver trays, and em*barr*ass the poor, who could only afford to bring wicker baskets to mourners' homes. For the sake of the poor, the law dictated that only baskets be used.

תנו רבנן: בראשונה היו מוליכין בבית האבל' עשירים – בקלתות של כסף ושל זהב' ועניים – בסלי נצרים של ערבה קלופה. והיו עניים מתביישים' התקינו שיהו הכל מביאין בסלי נצרים של ערבה קלופה' מפני כבודן של עניים. תנו רבנן: בראשונה היו משקין בבית האבל' עשירים – בזכוכית לבנה' ועניים בזכוכית צבועה' והיו עניים מתביישין. התקינו שיהו הכל משקין בזכוכית צבועה' מפני כבודן של עניים. בראשונה היו מגלין פני עשירים ומכסין פני עניים' מפני שהיו מושחרין פניהן מפני בצורת' והיו עניים מתביישין. התקינו שיהו מכסין פני הכל' מפני כבודן של עניים. בראשונה היו מוציאין עשירים בדרגש' ועניים בכליכה' והיו עניים מתביישין' התקינו שיהו הכל מוציאין בכליכה' מפני כבודן של עניים.

Our Rabbis taught: Formerly they used to serve drinks in a house of mourning, the rich in white glass vessels and the poor in colored glass, and the poor felt shamed; they instituted therefore that all should serve drinks in colored glass, out of deference to the poor. Formerly they used to uncover the face of the rich and cover the face of the poor, because their faces turned livid in years of drought and the poor felt shamed; they therefore instituted that everybody's face should be covered, out of deference to the poor. Formerly they used to bring out the rich [for burial] on an ornamented bed and the poor on a plain bier, and the poor felt shamed; they instituted therefore that all should be brought out on a plain bier, out of deference for the poor. (Mo'ed Katan 27a-b)

Our Rabbis taught: Formerly, they used to serve drinks in a house of mourning, the rich in white glass vessels and the poor in colored glass, and the poor felt shamed: they instituted therefore that all should serve drinks in colored glass, out of deference to the poor. Formerly they used to uncover the face of the rich and cover the face of the poor, because their faces turned livid in years of drought and the poor felt shamed; they therefore instituted that everybody's face should be covered, out of deference for the poor. Formerly they were used to bring out the rich [for burial] on an ornamented bed and the poor on a plain bier, and the poor felt shamed: they instituted therefore that all should be brought out on a plain bier, out of deference for the poor.

1.   **Can you differentiate between the actions discussed in the text that give dignity to the living and those that show honor for the dead?**

2.   **Moed Katan defines a principle that dictates much of Jewish practice in caring for the deceased until the time of burial and in comforting the mourners. What is that principle?**

3.   **Does this text show that the Rabbis wanted to honor the dead?**

4.   **Why did the decisions of the Rabbis in this text always favor the sensitivities of the poor?**

5.   **What do you think they were trying to say about the nature of death – and to some extent – about the nature of life?**

SHIVA

There are certain things the mourner must do during the first week after the burial, which is called *Shiva* (literally, seven) Notice that the week is counted from the burial, not from the death. These prescribed rules have in common the concretization of the abnormal situation of an individual suffering a loss. The mourner may not:

1.   Cut his hair.

2.   Wash his clothes.

3.   Wash himself carefully or wear cosmetics or perfumes.

4.   Have sexual intercourse.

5.   Wear leather shoes.

6.   Go to work.

7.   Study Torah (with some important exceptions—the mourner may study the Book of Jeremiah, who is called the "Prophet of Consolation" because he helped sustain the Jewish people through the destruction of Jerusalem and the First Temple; the Book of Job, which deals with the problem of good and evil; Lamentations, which describes poetically the destruction of Jerusalem; and the laws of mourning).

8. Sit on a regular chair or bed.

9. Have his head uncovered.

10. Greet anyone else.

Some of these traditions go back to ancient times, so it is difficult to know the reasons for them. We can guess at some. Non-leather shoes, for example, represent temporariness, and thus, symbolize the temporariness of life that would be on the mourner's mind. The prohibition of Torah study is based on the attitude that such activity is a source of joy and inspiration to the Jew. The books that are permitted all deal with various situations of mourning. The prohibition of greeting others, which applies even to dignitaries and scholars, represents our law's appreciation of the dignity of a mourner; he should not have to worry about etiquette at a time of great grief.

Emanuel Feldman, in an analysis of the laws of mourning entitled "Death as Estrangement,"[29] tries to tie these practices together:

> In effect, the law asks the mourner to behave as if he himself were dead. He is now an incomplete person, and his daily life begins to reflect the fact of his incompleteness. His physical appearance and his body are neglected. His relationship with God is interrupted. He has no commonality or community with other men. The qualities and characteristics of a living human being are suspended... In death, man has witnessed the opposite of life, of God, and of man, and he cannot now summarily leave death behind him and return quickly and easily into the land of the living.

> He knows now what it is to be without the breath of the God of life, and he can return to normal life and to renewed contact with the sacred only by degrees.

During *Shiva*, a candle is lit and left burning for all seven days. Light is the symbol of the soul, as suggested by the verse in the Book of Proverbs (20:27)

נֵר יְהֹוָה נִשְׁמַת אָדָם חֹפֵשׂ כָּל־חַדְרֵי־בָטֶן׃

The spirit of man is the lamp of the Lord.

As the flame is attached to the wick, so the soul is attached to the body.

Another tradition is to cover all of the mirrors in the mourner's house during *Shiva*. Again, there is no specific reason for this custom. One of the more relevant explanations is that the mirror is a symbol of human vanity which is out of place in a house of mourning.

Since the mourners stay home during *Shiva*, daily services are conducted in the house of mourning.

Shiva is cancelled if a holiday occurs in the middle of it. If the *Shiva* begins even one day before a festival, the entire *Shiva* is counted as if it were completed, through the one day. Should a death occur in the middle of the festival, the *Shiva* is postponed until after the holiday, and then the full seven days are observed.

---

[29] *(Riemer, Jewish Reflections on Death, p. 88.)*

On *Shabbat*, the mourning laws are suspended, but not cancelled. That means that no public forms of mourning are to be observed throughout the Sabbath. In the case of an out-of-town burial, those going with the casket begin *shiva* after the burial, while those staying behind begin when the casket is taken away.

During *Shiva*, mourners make their only appearance outside of the home during *Shabbat*. This occurs regardless of the day that *Shabbat* falls during *Shiva*. *Shabbat* and the urge to celebrate life supersede the desire and need to mourn the dead. In many congregations the mourners attend services, but do not enter the sanctuary at the start of *Kabbalat Shabbat*. Instead, they wait outside until after *Lecha Dodi*. Just before they begin Psalm 92, which officially ushers in *Shabbat*, the mourners are invited to enter. The worshippers greet them with the traditional words of condolence:

הַמָּקוֹם יְנַחֵם אֶתְכֶם בְּתוֹךְ שְׁאָר אֲבֵלֵי צִיוֹן וִירוּשָׁלָיִם

"May the Lord comfort you among the mourners of Zion and Jerusalem."

By appearing in the synagogue, the mourners begin to rejoin the community as participants and are not permitted to forget their obligations to include themselves as part of the community.

1. **Why do you think the mourners wait outside until after *Lecha Dodi*?**

2. **How does this sentence give comfort to mourners?**

3. **How do you feel when you say it?**

4. **How would you feel to hear someone else say it to you?**

5. **What do you notice about the words of condolence that the mourner is greeted with in regards to the community?**

NIHUM AVELIM

It is also a *mitzvah* to visit the family during the entire first week following the burial. There are many customs regulating such a visitation. Unfortunately, most people do not know what to do in the house of a mourner, and often, we find an almost festive atmosphere present.

Visiting a house where someone is sitting *shiva* or encountering someone who has recently lost a relative can be an awkward experience. What do you say to a mourner? Do you need to say anything or is just being there enough?

The visit can take the form of helping with the chores in the Shiva house (something that the mourner in his present condition may find difficult to do), joining in the religious services that are usually conducted in a house of mourning, or just sitting in silence showing by one's mere presence that he shares the sorrow of the mourner. Leave it to the mourner to speak first.

אָמַר רַבִּי יוֹחָנָן: אֵין מְנַחֲמִין רַשָּׁאִין לוֹמַר דָּבָר עַד שִׁיפְתַּח אָבֵל'

Rabbi Yohanan said, "Comforters are not permitted to say a word until the mourner begins the conversations." (Mo'ed Katan 28b)

The purpose of visiting the mourner is not to make him feel better or to forget his loss. The whole concept of *Nihum Avelim* (comforting the mourners) is to have the mourner discuss his feelings and bring them out into the open. The "comforters" should be solemn and quiet. They shouldn't avoid the issue. Chances are that the mourner is looking for the opportunity of talking about his loved one. Crying is, in fact, to be encouraged. The visitors should even ask about the deceased. It is only by getting these feelings out that the mourner can hope to regain his sense of normalcy and acceptance of the death. By engaging in laughter or becoming distracted, the mourner may feel relieved for the moment, but it is a short-lived escape. He may appear consoled in the presence of guests, but is left with a real void after they leave.

It is also acceptable to share stories of the deceased with the mourner. This may, in fact, be one of the reasons for *Shiva*. It creates an opportunity for the mourner to learn more about the person being mourned.

If people wish to bring gifts, they may do so, but care should be taken that the gift fits the occasion. The most appropriate gift prevalent today is a contribution to the deceased's favorite charity or to the synagogue where she or he worshipped.

1. **How do you pick a *tzedakah* (i.e. is it reflective of their values)?**

2. **When giving *tzedakah* as a tribute to someone who has passed away, do you respect the wishes of the family and give to the *tzedakah* that they have picked or to your favorite?**

3. **Do you ever feel obligated to speak when visiting a mourner? Why?**

4. **Why do you think Jewish tradition insists on specific mourning practices and behaviors in comforting mourners?**

5. **Wouldn't it be best simply to allow every mourner and comforting visitor to do what they want to do naturally?**

SHLOSHIM

It is the recognition that man can return to normalcy only by degrees, only through a gradual process, that created the laws of mourning. The next degree after *shiva* is called *shloshim* (literally, thirty). This period covers the entire first month following the burial. In this period, the mourner already comes out of the house, returns to work, and gets back into a daily routine. However, he continues to refrain from cutting his hair, and from joining festive celebrations. Since music is considered a manifestation of festivity, the mourner should remove himself from a room in which music is being played or listened to. The end of *shloshim* marks the end of mourning for all relatives except parents.

SHANA/ KADDISH PERIOD

When a child is mourning for a parent, the restrictions of the *Shloshim* period are extended for twelve months. *Kaddish* is recited during the morning, afternoon, and evening services, for eleven months. Originally the period for this was twelve months, based on the idea that the memory of the deceased is fresh in the mind for twelve months. It was reduced to eleven months because twelve months was regarded as the maximum period of punishment for the wicked by the heavenly court, and should the mourner say *Kaddish* for twelve months, it would suggest that the child considered his parent as deserving the maximum penalty. The custom of reciting *Kaddish* only eleven months has remained, even if the original reason is less compelling today.

YAHRZEIT

The next stage is the first anniversary of the death, called *Yahrzeit* (Yiddish, literally meaning, "year time"). On the *Yahrzeit*, it is customary to light a special memorial candle that burns for 24 hours. The mourner will attend services and recite the *Kaddish*. This is done every year on the anniversary of the death. In some congregations, the mourner will be called to the Torah for an *aliyah* on the *Shabbat* prior to the *Yarzheit*. The Memorial Prayer, *El Malei Rachamim*, will be recited. If the mourner does not know the exact day of the death, he should choose a day and keep it as the permanent Yarzheit.

TOMBSTONES

וַיַּצֵּב יַעֲקֹב מַצֵּבָה עַל־קְבֻרָתָהּ הִוא מַצֶּבֶת קְבֻרַת־רָחֵל עַד־הַיּוֹם:

Over her grave Jacob set up a pillar; it is the pillar at Rachel's grave to this day. (Bereishit 35:20)

After burying Rachel, Jacob erected a monument over her grave. From this developed our tradition of placing a marker to identify the grave so that relatives can find it when they visit and to honor the memory of the deceased.

While there is really no hard and fast rule about when the monument should be erected, it has become customary to do so at the end of one year, since erecting it earlier would suggest that the memory of the deceased is fading, and artificial means become necessary to keep it alive.

Our custom is to place the monument at the head of the grave. The name of the deceased and the date of death are inscribed on the tombstone. In the past, it was customary to have elaborate inscriptions, but today the tendency is toward simplicity. The inscription contains the name of the deceased in English and Hebrew - the way he was called to the Torah, i.e., by first name and his father's (and, sometimes, mother's) name - and in the local language, the date of death according to both the Jewish and secular calendars.

Sometimes above this inscription one finds two Hebrew letters, פ"נ, which are the initials for פה נקבר, "Here Lies." The Sephardim use the letters מ"ק standing for מצבת קבר, meaning "Monument of the grave of." Underneath the inscription one usually finds the letters תנצב"ה standing for *"May his soul be bound up in the bond of eternal life."*

UNVEILING

It has become the custom to "unveil" the tombstone, accompanied by a religious service. The name comes from the practice of covering the tombstone with a cloth which is removed at the service by members of the family. They thus "unveil" the monument. The unveiling usually takes place a year after the death.

While there is no authority for this service in tradition - except that it was the custom to visit the graves on the day of the *Yahrzeit* (and in some families, before *Rosh HaShanah* or one's wedding day) - it is now an accepted and meaningful practice. It is, however, not at all mandatory or necessary. It is certainly not necessary for a rabbi to officiate, although families usually request a Rabbi's presence. It does offer another opportunity to pay tribute to the deceased and to speak to the living about the meaning of life and death. Caution should be used not to allow this to become a social event.

The practices and views outlined above give some insights into Jewish attitudes relating to death. Many observances and feelings involve complicated laws and circumstances, which should be considered with the advice of your rabbi.

Discussion

1. **An important bit of North American Jewish history is that in almost every town, the first institution created was a burial society—even before a synagogue. Why?**

2. **The Kaddish does not mention death at all. How did it become identified with mourning?**

How are the Jewish mourning rituals...

Something that helps me heal	Something that tied me to tradition	Something that made me feel important	Something that helps Jewish unity

GUIDE TO THE *HEVRAH KADDISHA*

Adopted by the Committee on Congregational Standards

October 27, 1965

Reviewed June 1998

Preamble: the Guide to the *Hevrah Kadisha* is to be regarded as complementary to the Guide to Funeral Practices of the United Synagogue. The *Hevrah Kaddisha* is the name given to the congregational committee or organization whose purpose it is to perform the *mitzvah* of preparing the deceased for burial in accordance with the Jewish tradition. The following suggestions are presented to all our congregations in the hope that they may prove helpful to those *Hevrut Kadisha* now functioning as well as to new ones which may be formed.

COMPOSITION OF THE HEVRAH KADISHA

1. The *Hevrah Kadisha* shall be a standing committee of the congregation functioning under the guidance of and with the cooperation of the Rabbi and *Hazan*. In some congregations, the *Hevrah Kadisha* is a separate corporation though legally associated with the congregation.

2. Congregations may find it advisable to join with other congregations in forming a common *Hevrah Kadisha* to serve all associated for this purpose.

3. The *Hevrah Kadisha* should be a committee distinct and apart from the Cemetery Committee. Where such separation is not feasible, the committees may be merged.

4. The duties of the *Hevrah Kadisha* are among the most important *mitzvot* incumbent upon us. Membership should be regarded as a distinct honor carrying with it the appreciation and respect of the entire congregation. Members of the Hevrah Kadisha include men and women who serve and perform their duties willingly and piously.

In some congregations, members of the *Hevrah Kadisha* are honored annually by a special congregational dinner, usually on the seventh day of the Hebrew month of Adar, the *Yahrzeit* of Moses and the traditional day for the annual meeting and *Seudat Mitzvah* of the *Hevrah Kadisha*.

THE DUTIES OF THE HEVRAH KADISHA

A. INITIAL ARRANGEMENTS

1. In the areas where there are Jewish funeral establishments, the *Hevrah Kadisha* stands in readiness to arrange for the funeral of the deceased, the date and the hour, in consultation with the bereaved family, the Rabbi and the *Hazan*.

2. In areas where there are no Jewish funeral establishments, the *Hevrah Kadisha* shall, with permission, relieve the family of this task and together with the Rabbi and *Hazan* make the arrangements itself.

B. TAHARAH

1. The *Hevrah Kadisha* shall arrange for the *Taharah*, the ritual washing of the body. The *Taharah* rite should preferably be performed by members of the *Hevrah Kadisha*. This is the practice in most *Hevrot Kadisha*. Where this is not possible, persons hired especially for this purpose may be used.

2. *Tachrichim* (white linen shrouds) shall be used to clothe the deceased. Other garments shall not be used. This is in keeping with the Jewish tradition that in death all are equal.

3. Every adult male shall, in addition to the *tachrichim*, be buried with a *kipah* and a *talit* which has been rendered *pasul*, namely in a *talit* from which one fringe has been removed.

C. SHOMRIM

1. A Jewish tradition requires that the deceased be attended to continuously from the moment of death until burial and that his/her memory be honored by the reading of Psalms during the night before the funeral by *shomrim* (watchers).

D. THE FUNERAL

2. Interment traditionally occurs no later than one day after death. The Rabbi should be consulted about exceptional circumstances.

3. To emphasize the equality in all of death, Jewish tradition calls for simplicity and bars ostentatious display. The Guide to Funeral Practices of the United Synagogue should be consulted and followed.

4. The *Hevrah Kadisha* shall offer assistance in arranging for a burial plot in conjunction with the Cemetery Committees.

E. PERIOD OF MOURNING

1. During the *Shivah* period, the *Hevrah Kadisha* or other appropriate committee shall assure wherever possible that a *minyan* convenes morning and evening at the home of the mourner.

2. It should provide prayer books, *talitot*, *kipot* and *tefillin*.

BIBLIOGRAPHY AND REFERENCE

Portions of this text were excerpted from the following texts, used with permission. Ritual practices and procedures were excerpted from _Moreh Derekh_: The Rabbi's Manual of the Rabbinical Assembly, used with permission.

Abelson, Kass and David Fine, editors. Responsa 1991-2000. New York: The Rabbinical Assembly, 2002.

Astor, Carl. _M'shaneh Habriot_: Who Makes People Different. New York: United Synagogue of Conservative Judaism, Department of Youth Activities, 1985.

Cytron, Barry and Earl Schwartz. When Life is in the Balance: Life and Death Decisions in Light of Jewish Tradition. New York: United Synagogue of Conservative Judaism, Department of Youth Activities, 1994.

Dorff, Elliott. This is My Beloved, This is My Friend: A Rabbinic Letter on Intimate Relations. New York: The Rabbinical Assembly 1996.

Feldman, David. The Jewish Family Relationship. New York: United Synagogue of Conservative Judaism, Department of Youth Activities, 1975.

Gordis, Daniel. _Am Kadosh_: Celebrating Our Uniqueness. New York, United Synagogue of Conservative Judaism, Department of Youth Activities, 1992.

Klein, Isaac. A Time to Be Born, A Time to Die. New York: United Synagogue of Conservative Judaism, Department of Youth Activities, 1988.

Novick, Bernard. _B'Tzelem Elohim_: In God's Image. New York: United Synagogue of Conservative Judaism, Department of Youth Activities, 1998.

Rank, Perry and Gordon Freeman, editors. _Moreh Derekh_: The Rabbi's Manual of The Rabbinical Assembly. New York: The Rabbinical Assembly, 1998.

Steinberg, Barbara and Dara Zabb. _Tzorchei Tzibbur_: Community and Responsibility in the Jewish Tradition. New York: United Synagogue of Conservative Judaism, Department of Youth Activities, 1999.

Wasser, Joel. We Are Family. New York: United Synagogue of Conservative Judaism, Department of Youth Activities, 1991.